INTERNATIONAL LAW
and the
BLACK MINORITY
IN THE U.S.

by

Y. N. Kly

D1293825

CLARITY

Copyright © 1985 Yussuf Naim Kly

ISBN: 0-932863-01-9
LCCN: 85-073906

First published simultaneously by Clarity Press, Inc., Atlanta, and
Commoners' Publishing Society, Inc., Ottawa, Canada. (ISBN: 0-
88970-065-6)

Third Edition: 1990

In-house Editor: Diana G. Collier

Cataloging in Publication Data:

Kly, Yussuf Naim
    International law and the Black minority in the U.S.

ISBN: 0-88970-065-6

1. Civil rights (international law)
2. Afro-Americans - Civil rights. I. Title.

3X4231.M5K49 1986 323.4   C86-090071-1

CLARITY PRESS, INC.
Suite 469, 3277 Roswell Rd. N.E.
Atlanta, GA. 30305, USA

and

CLARITY INTERNATIONAL
P.O. Box 3144
Windsor, Ont. N8N 2M3, Canada

TABLE OF CONTENTS

FOREWORD

This work is prepared to be of interest to all Americans as well as to other citizens of multi-national countries. To Anglo-Americans, whose historical action through the past centuries is a witness to their sharp and undisputed awareness of collective rights in relation to themselves, this research serves as a reminder that other groups also have such rights equal to theirs, though not necessarily the same. For Afro-Americans, whose awareness of their human rights seems somewhat doubtful, this work hopes to provide a comparative measurement of their situation outside of the recent slave/freed slave measurement presently in widespread use. Also other multi-national states seeking models for their domestic use may see in this book a descriptive, objective demystification of the U.S. model, better allowing them to evaluate its advantages and disadvantages (cost/benefit) for application to their national minority problems.

This book points to a fourth option, one apart from nationalism, assimilation or self-determination, that does not deny the possibility of these options, while still encouraging national unity. The fourth option is to investigate the international norms for realistic sincere examples of how such options are implemented within the context of state unity and progressive development, and how much, and under which circumstances an option becomes legally required or feasible.

In this book, we use the term "minority" as meaning the same as "nationality", when there is more than one nationality within a state, and at least one of those nationalities is dominant over the other(s). We also often use the American-instituted term "affirmative action" synonymously with the less particularized and more scientific term, "special measures." This is done to help bring the U.S.-used term closer to its international law meaning, thus broadening it not only to approve of quotas, but also of any other special measure or affirmative action that is required to achieve the equal status of the minority. Thus a program for assimilation, integration or self-determination is also affirmative action or special measures—if chosen and necessary.

The constant need to correspond U.S. domestic terminology with international law terminology so that a standard objective non-self-serving definition of terms can be achieved is an active reminder of why the question of national minority protection has been and must always be primarily an international responsibility as well as a domestic obligation.

Above all, the reader of this book must understand that international norms and principles for the treatment of national minorities have developed and been accepted by nations for decades. It is these norms that this work describes and compares to the U.S. norms. It is these norms that have become a part of international law through treaties and membership in the U.N. implicitly a voluntary submission of a degree of sovereignty), and hence part of the laws of all states.

When such laws are not followed by a nation, it is not truly constructive to say that legitimate law makers such as the U.N. or World Court have no power to enforce the law because any individual nation has more guns than they. Rather, it is more realistic to ask how long can a nation continue policies such as forced assimilation, which are internationally inacceptable and illegal? Acquiescence to just law is the most powerful and important means by which people and nations are able to communicate and cooperate.

Lastly, we have often used the term "domestic colonialism" without elaborating on its meaning and dimensions. This is due to the fact that the root purpose of this book is to describe minority rights in international law. It is in the process of comparing the notion of minority rights in international law with the historical notion of minority rights in the U.S. that we are consistently confronted with the paradox that the U.S., even given its notion of minority rights as meaning civil rights and assimilation, in actual historical practice treats its national minorities in a manner which often corresponds to the constituent elements of imperialism and colonialism: *domination, exploitation, and inequality.* This paradox has led to the question of whether the U.S. minority rights system actually permits a system of domestic colonialism or imperialism. Keeping within the context of the purposes of this book, we feel no need to do more than raise the question to the extent to which the purposes of this book would require.

Viewing the problem of minorities within a context of priority emphasis on national unity or on Anglo-American privileges is in reality a subjective perspective which prevents the realization of the effects of the objective facts on the condition of the minority. Therefore, such a subjective perspective may in itself be causal to the oppressive condition of minorities.

International law is becoming an increasingly viable alternative used by enlightened states to achieve national interest goals through the establishment of principles and rules by which the dragon of power politics can be harnessed in such a manner that its long term effects are not more damaging to the nation-state's interest than its short term gains.[1] The editorial in *Journal of International Law,* (Vol. 70, 1976, pp. 1-27), states:

The study of international law is rapidly becoming one of the cutting edges of the discipline of International Relations. As a result of increasing global interdependence, the interactions of states are tending more and more to center around such matters as peacekeeping, environmental pollution, uses of the sea, international trade and commercial policy (including the activities of multinational enterprises) and human and minority rights. In pursuing policy objectives relating to these matters, governments are relying increasingly on the international legal process.

Individual nations, groups of nations, international organizations, individuals and groups are finding that international law is indispensable for influencing events in directions which serve their interest.[2] In this way, international law in general may be thought of as a body of international standards or norms by which nations and other international personalities outwardly judge the fairness of each others' actions, thus tending to convert political struggles into legalistic and peaceful argumentation. This occurs in a manner similar to the way the United Nations' organs make possible the converting of certain violent struggles into non-violent political struggles. In some cases, legal arguments are more amenable to solution than are open political confrontations,[3] the reason being that, in the process of accepting or feeling obliged to accept a legalistic approach, each nation involved automatically agrees to accept certain common definitions of goals and values.

Of course, just as all problems among nations cannot be resolved through peaceful political processes, neither can all problems be submitted to international law. Indeed, one might say that in today's world, most problems cannot be solved through the international law alternative alone. Indeed, most solutions today come through a mixture of political, military and judicial processes, each indispensable to the process of solution. However, there seems to be an increasing willingness among nation-states to center many aspects of their interactions around questions of international law. Due to the present and future systemic regulatory potential that the colonialism: domination, exploitation, and inequality". Thus, the U.S. view of minority rights permits a system of domestic colonialism in violation of contemporary international human rights law, most particularly the general principles embodied in Article 27 of the United Nations Covenant on Civil and Political Rights. This central text of international human rights law states: "In those states in which ethnic, religious or linguistic minorities exist, persons belonging to such minorities shall not be denied the right, in community with the members of their group, to enjoy their own culture, to profess and practice their own religion, or to use their own language."

Kly argues that Article 27 requires that a government grant official recognition to its national minorities and special measures for them. Until the United States accepts these two obligations, Kly asserts, the credibility of U.S. human rights foreign policy and solutions to the problems of blacks and other minorities in the United States will continue to be impeded.

Part I of Kly's book elaborates the international law concept of minority collective rights, citing Switzerland, a country with three national minorities, French, Italian and Romanche, spread out among the 25 cantons of the Swiss confederation, as an example of a modern Western state that has instituted effective minority protection institutions. Besides the concrete example of the multilingual Swiss state, Kly sketches a brief history of minority rights in Western state practice, beginning with the 17th and 18th centuries, when a number of treaties between European countries incorporated clauses relating to the rights of religious minorities. This process continued and developed through the 19th and early 20th centuries, culminating in Article 27, "the essence," according to Kly, of the ILVCR.

Part 2 analyzes the U.S. concept of collective rights of minorities and its divergence from the ILVCR. Kly's survey of the history of black-white relations in America is divided into four parts: the slavery period (1776-1865), Reconstruction (1868-1895), the apartheid period (1895-1960) and the era of Martin Luther King, Jr. (1960-1975). It leads him to conclude that there has never existed any clear-cut, legally articulated minority policy in the United States, certainly not one that would meet the requirements of official recognition and special measures mandated by Article 27 and international human rights law. Instead, Kly argues, the USVCR is "highly flexible and pragmatic", thus assuring that the "maxim that majority self-interest will prevail over minority rights is in no danger of becoming antiquated." Suggesting that legislative initiatives such as the 1964 and 1968 Civil Rights Acts were but "a pragmatic response intended merely to stave off further minority protest," Kly joins a growing chorus of black and other American intellectuals of color who have offered negative assessments of the civil rights movement of the recent past and of the prospects for improvements in race relations in the United States for the near future (see for example, Derrick Bell's new book, *And We Are Not Saved {1987}).* Kly's unique contribution is to place the past, present and future of U.S. race relations within the broader context of international human rights law, thus permitting an assessment of the USVCR of minorities according to the evolving norms of a legal discourse on national minorities liberated from a history of "international enslavement, extermination and gross exploitation." Kly's strategic placement of the USVCR within the more widely accepted normative discourse of international human rights law provides not only an alternative vision of race relations in the United States, but also, even more importantly, an alternative *solution.* Kly's unique perspective is worthy of consideration and debate by minority and non-minority individuals alike, intrigued by the possibility that the rule of law is more likely to be discovered in universal declarations of human rights than in more parochial interpretations.

ROBERT A. WILLIAMS, Jr.
University of Arizona / Lumbee Indian Tribe*

* First appeared as a review in *The American Journal of International Law,* Vol. 82, 1988, pp. 688-690.

PART ONE

THE INTERNATIONAL LAW CONCEPT OF COLLECTIVE RIGHTS IN RELATION TO NATIONAL MINORITIES

INTRODUCTION

The increasing frequency of newspaper headlines denoting minority-majority conflicts within nation-states as threats to international peace,[5] national development, and healthy relations among nations, is a convincing sign that the problems of minorities in small and large states demand urgent attention. The colonial divisions of Africa and Asia, which serve today as geographical boundaries for the modern nation-states of these regions, as well as the forced transportation of Africans to America and later, the economically-coerced emigration of Africans and Asians to Europe, will contribute to future international crises.[6] Majority-minority problems exist also in the more developed nations of Europe, in Canada and in the U.S..[7]

Apparently the success of the U.S., through the systematic use of racism and discrimination, in creating an almost impenetrable form of domestic capitalist colonialism based primarily on racial rather than geographic boundary lines was, like other American technologies, transferred to Europe, particularly England, which, having just lost most of the colonial territories and having had its efforts at neocolonialism exposed even before decolonialization itself was completed, quickly saw the advantages of adopting a method of domestic colonialism which had evolved so admirably in the U.S.. Thus capitalists in Europe encouraged large numbers of skilled and unskilled labor from Africa and Asia to emigrate, knowing full well that the white racist orientation of western European societies, particularly in England, would place these minorities, *vis-à-vis* the majority, in a position similar to the black and Asian minorities in the U.S.. This focus on Western Europe does not, however, ignore the fact that non-European capitalists and dictators the world over have sought to benefit feudal and capitalist development through the exploitation of national minorities. The importance of emphasizing the problem in the U.S. and western Europe is not because it is unique to these countries, but because of the important role that the U.S. and western Europe play in the shaping of international law and the international machinery necessary to expose and eliminate domestic colonialism.

In his article, "The Transnational Protection of Ethnic Minorities: a Tentative Framework for Enquiry", Professor J. Claydon of Queen's University cites more than 25 cases where minority problems may create difficulties for international peace. He emphasizes the importance of these problems for international relations, and predicts that the next decade will see an upsurge in minority rights-induced crises.[8] Numerous other social scientists have recently emphasized the importance of international minority protection for the maintenance of world peace and development: Y. Dinstein,[9] R. Hauser,[10] Claude L. Inis.[11] In his article "National Minorities in International Law", Professor Kelly of the Dickinson School of Law observed:

> ...Since World War 11 the issue of minorities has remained relatively dormant... however the various conditions which directly caused this neglect have either disappeared or are changing; minority groups are increasingly asserting their right to existence and protection, and the basic international machinery is once more available to respond to their problems... With the rapid decline of colonialism following World War 11, and the concurrent emergence of nation-states all over the world, the world minorities locked within the boundaries of states have increased... Violence and terrorism have marked the path of minorities as they have had to fend for themselves in the absence of any international commission or treaty system; for example... the Kurds of Iraq, the Nagas of Northeastern India... the tribes of Upper Burma, the Huks and Islamic tribes of the Philippines... the French Canadians, and the Basque of Northwestern Spain have all been unsuccessful in their efforts... The Irish Catholics of Northern Ireland and the Palestinian Arabs are in the throes of a violent struggle for political identity, with only partial success to date... It appears that the future of minorities may lie, where independence is not possible, in a form of (political) autonomy within the particular nation-state concerned, where the members may both maintain their cultural heritage and participate fully in the benefits of the larger society.[12]

The problems of minorities are of particular importance to scholars of international human rights law because a prime reason for the existence of this discipline is to establish principles whereby rules for the harmonious and peaceful relationship among groups may evolve and be discerned. The sacredness of the ethnic idea, of the right of a people to continue to be themselves in all significant ways in which their culture has made them distinguishable and unique from other ethnies, has found recognition in the principles of 20th century human rights law, in the instruments for minority protection in the constitutions of progressive and socialist nations, and in international bodies including the United Nations. In order to present a fuller picture of the troublesome political potential of the collective rights problem as it concerns minorities and U.S. minorities in particular, we will first present a broad view of the historical evolution of the minority problem in relation to changing power relations in the international system; then we will examine how major powers influence the human rights output of the law-determining organs of the United Nations, thus influencing international law, specifically as it relates to collective rights of minorities.

Historical Overview

Ethnic self-awareness (the genesis of the minority problem)[13] emerged slowly, despite the existence of the many ethnies within the pre-World War I European empires. As Ernest Barker noted:

> The self-consciousness of nations is a product of the nineteenth century... Nations were already there... but it is not the things which are simply 'there' that matter in human life... In the world of action, apprehended ideas are alone electrical; and a nation must be an idea as well as a fact before it can become a dynamic force.[14]

Before the French revolution, popular notions of creating ethnically-delineated states were not entertained in Europe. Though there were some demands for an Italian state following the Napoleonic experience, these ideas found little acceptance until the 'Risorgimento' movement in the middle of the 19th century.[15] Instead, the period before and shortly after the French revolution was marked by the paradoxical belief within Europe that, while political control by the acknowledged leader of a foreign national group was unacceptable, rule by an otherwise foreign prince was quite acceptable.[16] It was after 1831 that Europe began to experience movements that were totally unambiguous in their linkage to ethnic consciousness and power politics. The Italians', Hungarians' and Germans' revolutions of 1848, although ending in failure, indicated how rapidly the ethnic dogma of self-determination or nationalism was spreading. Even the movements which were successfully suppressed, such as the Irish and Polish uprisings, were elevated to become the Irish question, the Polish question.

By the eve of the First World War, ethnic nationalism was a major factor in European development. This factor was accordingly reflected in the postwar creation of the League of Nations. The high degree of self-awareness among national minorities in Europe played a key role in determining the emphasis which the League placed on minority protection in its search for world peace and security. The constitutional and international legal minority protection devices for national minorities or emigrant minorities found in Europe today result not only from the power relations which existed between majorities and national minorities in European nation-states, but also from the degree to which the question of national minorities was consequently elevated to a level of international concern and law *(jus aquum)* in the League of Nations. It is well to note that the League's machinery was primarily developed to protect national minorities generally of the same racial and geographic background as the majority, not the immigrant or enslaved minorities of African and Asian racial and geographic background. In this forum, U.S. President Woodrow Wilson helped popularize the expression 'the right of self-determination', which had been coined by Karl Marx.[17] Wilson and his contemporaries, however, never envisaged its use on a non-European scale where,[18] as we shall see, Marx's concept of self-determination was to be applied on a global scale and play an important role in the U.S.S.R.'s global strategy, especially after World War II.

After the Second World War, the power relations in the international system underwent a dramatic change. Postwar European history was dominated by the efforts of the European countries to rebuild their politico-economic structure following the destructions of World War 11. These efforts coincided with the foreign policy objectives of Britain and America of preventing the possible expansion of the Soviet Union or communism into western Europe. As American economic and military assistance were seen as requisite to achieve these objectives, and were subsequently forthcoming through the Marshall Plan and the establishment of the NATO treaty and operations, America became involved on the European continent to such an extent that she appropriated the initiative in continental policy formulation. American and British influence combined led to German rearmament and to the creation of the international alliances of NATO, OEEC, WEU, as a counter to the Warsaw Pact nations.

The shift of power following World War II from Britain, France, Italy, Germany and Japan, to the new world powers, the U.S. and the U.S.S.R., led to the existence between 1948-1954 of what scholars often refer to as a bipolar international system, divided between Eastern Europe (the Soviet bloc) and western Europe and America (the Atlantic community). While the U.S.S.R.was emerging as second in power to the U.S., the U.S. was definitely the dominant power in the world. As Dennis Meadows noted in speaking of American power:

> ... le pouvoir, elle l'exerce aussi bien évidemment, par la puissance de son économie. En 1950, le produit national brut des E.-U. est plus de deux fois superieur à celui de l'Allemagne, du Japon, de la Grande Bretagne, de la France et de l'Italie reunis: 288 milliards de dollars contre 117.19

Most importantly however, the U.S. had without a doubt the greatest military potential. Her political influence in all international organizations outside of the Soviet bloc, including the U.N. and NATO,20 was a natural concomitant to her tremendous military and economic power.

Just as the League of Nations reflected the predominant concerns and policy orientations of the European nations who dominated the world scene at its creation, so too did the new United Nations, created after World War 11, reflect the new international order. The minority rights question, which had received pre-eminent attention in the League, was de-emphasized in the U.N., largely due to America's concept of human rights.21 During this period 1948-54, the greater part of the U.S. chief minority, the blacks, lived in the southern states under an American form of what can only be called racial apartheid. Although this chief minority, at this point, had developed no power position *vis-à-vis* the dominant Anglo-Americans from which it could bargain for recognition of rights, the black national minority along with the Indian, Spanish of the southwest, and a host of immigrant minorities, represented a potential hornet's nest which the U.S. had no desire to risk disturbing by furthering egalitarian concepts internationally which might someday serve to alter its traditional slave and conquest-oriented minority development.22 Thus, vulnerable on the domestic front as far as collective rights in relation to minorities were concerned, the U.S. embarked upon a policy of de-emphasizing collective human rights in the U.N. in favor of an emphasis on individual civil and political human rights.

However, as Soviet power and influence represented a counter to American might in the new international order, so too has it served to counter American de-emphasis of collective human rights in the U.N..23

Having perceived that by lessening tensions and avoiding conflict in Europe, she would heighten the European powers' awareness of their political and economic differences with America and thus weaken the Atlantic Alliance, the U.S.S.R. focussed its foreign policy initiatives on avoiding confrontations in Europe while encouraging independence movements by colonized 'peoples' of the Third World. This Soviet strategy, which opened the way to the process of decolonization, was reflected in the U.N. by a new emphasis on collective rights and in particular, on the political right of self-determination.[24]

During the period 1958-1977, the international system saw the beginning of a relative decline in the U.S. moral model and the attractiveness of the U.S. as an economic and socio-political model. Several setbacks, the assassination of Kennedy under unclear circumstances, the minority riots or insurrections in more than 150 major American cities, the murder of Martin Luther King, the shooting of students on university campuses, the rise of crime and violence in large cities, the drug problem, and above all, the Vietnam war and the Iranian and Lebanese failures subsequently, had weakened world confidence in the desirability and invincibility of the American socio-political and economic system.

The consequent weakening of U.S. influence in the U.N. occurred concomitantly with a rise in influence of the Third World, pan-Islamic and socialist blocs. The late 70's saw the near completion of the decolonization process, and a new influx of Third World nations to membership in the General Assembly. With its numerical (voting) power thus increased, the socialist/Third World bloc was able to shift Assembly attention to matters of its immediate concern, and to pass resolutions which previously would have been stymied by U.S. opposition. Accordingly, the late 70's and early 80's saw the passage of numerous resolutions in the U.N. directly concerned with self-determination and collective human rights in general, as well as the withdrawal of the U.S. from UNESCO and the ILO.

Power Politics and Collective Rights in the U.N.

Thus far we have suggested that power politics influences the action of states in the U.N., which is, along with its International Court of Justice, an important law-creating and interpreting agency. This means that major powers tend to have a disproportionately higher influence on what other states accept as rules and principles in the U.N., on how these rules and principles are interpreted, and on what is emphasized. In this manner, major powers may disproportionately influence the law-creating and law-determining sources and thus human rights law itself.[25] In order to interpret the effect of power politics on the law-influencing resolutions, etc. of the U.N. as it concerns minorities, we have examined the human rights emphasis of both socialist and western liberal countries as it concerns collective rights. We have found that collective rights as it concerns minorities are chiefly promoted by the socialist bloc in accordance with their domestic and international ideologies, and that collective rights are chiefly de-emphasized by the U.S. along with other members of the western liberal bloc.[26] We have also found that the capacity of each major power bloc to exert influence in the U.N. was related to their relative power position in the international system, that is, that their period of maximal influence in U.N. output coincides with their period of maximum strength in the international system. It is only in recent years, as the socialist bloc gained in power relative to the western democracies, that collective rights have taken on special importance in the U.N.. This can be vividly illustrated by a short historical review of U.N. procedures concerning human rights.

Early in 1946, the first Human Rights Commission, consisting of Nationalist China, France, Lebanon, Australia, Byelorussia, Chile, Egypt, India, Panama, the Philippines, the U.S.S.R., the United Kingdom, the U.S.A., Uruguay and Yugoslavia, was established.[27] Of the fifteen countries mentioned, only three belonged to the socialist bloc. During the first meeting of the Commission, under the chairmanship of the late Mrs. E. Roosevelt, the United Kingdom presented a draft international bill of rights. Both the U.S. and U.S.S.R., the major powers of the postwar era, took a critical stance and their combined power prevailed. They felt that it would be premature to discuss any measures that would have binding force. Thus, this disagreement was resolved by the U.N. decision to have two major documents, one a declaration of the general principles (the Universal Declaration of Human Rights) and the other a covenant which was to have binding obligations. The decision or compromise permitted the major powers (the U.S. and U.S.S.R.) to immediately sign the Universal Declaration of Human Rights, which had a non-binding character, while leaving the covenant, which was to have binding character, for later consideration. The Universal Declaration was adopted by the General Assembly on December 10, 1948.

The political division along ideological lines, as it relates to collective rights, emerged in the United Nations between the socialist and western bloc on December 10, 1948.[28] It can be seen in the difference in focus between the U.S. and U.S.S.R. concerning the thirty articles of the Universal Declaration. Articles 1 and 2 were general in nature, asserting that all human beings are born free and equal in dignity and rights, and that all are entitled to the rights and freedoms set forth in the Declaration, regardless of race, color, sex, language, religion, political or other opinion, national or social origin, property, birth or other status. Articles 3 to 22 express the general U.S. liberal emphasis on individual civil and political rights: the right to life, liberty and security; the right to equal protection of the law; the right to a fair trial; the right to freedom of movement and residence within a country, and to leave and return to it; the right to a nationality; the right to property; the right to freedom of thought; the right to freedom of opinion and expression, etc.. Articles 22 to 27 deal with the concepts usually emphasized by socialist countries of collective social and economic rights: the right to work under just and favourable conditions; the right to equal pay for equal work; the right to rest and leisure; the right to a standard of living adequate for health and wellbeing; the right to education; the right to participate freely in the cultural life of the community, etc.. This political division necessitated the drafting of two covenants instead of one: the Covenant of Civil and Political Rights, promoted primarily by the western block, and the Covenant on Social and Economic Rights promoted primarily by the U.S.S.R. and socialist bloc countries.

It is interesting to note that while both the U.S. and the U.S.S.R. felt that the right of self-determination was important, the U.S. viewed self-determination in the sense of the Woodrow Wilson Doctrine, ie. not as it applied to the U.S. or its western Allies, but rather as it was interpreted to apply to the Ottoman and Austrian empires and to the "nations behind the Iron Curtain."[29] The U.S.S.R. tended to view self-determination in accordance with its foreign policy objective of weakening the western alliance or capitalist nations by assisting colonial territories to obtain their political independence.

At the beginning of the post World War II period, U.N. resolutions and institutions sponsored by the western countries were most often adopted. The U.S. and western countries fostered classical liberal international institutions such as the International Bank, the International Monetary Fund, the International Court of Justice, GATT; promoted classical liberal ideological concepts such as the network of bilateral treaties on traditional liberal economic subjects (relief from double taxation, protection for investments against confiscatory expropriations, the right to exploit the resources of the continental shelf); and reoriented international laws of national transportation towards the needs of central, modern capitalist industrial development.

However, in recent years, with the changes in international power relations favoring the U.S.S.R. as a result primarily of the failure of western policy to meet the needs of the Third World, the United Nations has begun to adopt more resolutions and institutions in conformity with Third World and socialist interest. The U.S.S.R. and its socialist allies have successfully presented themselves as the champion of "oppressed peoples" in the United Nations. They have supported the legal, political and military fights against colonialism in Asia and Africa, and waged a verbal duel for minority rights in the U.S. and western Europe. To this point, a socialist scholar writes:

It cannot be accepted that in certain capitalist countries, democrats and communists are prevented from following their profession. Sometimes progressive forces are even witch-hunted, as happened in the case of Angela Davis. Likewise not in conformity with human rights is the oppression of 'Negroes', Puerto-Ricans and Indians in the United States of America. The 250 Indians who in spring of 1972 defended their rights at Wounded Knee can count on the sympathy of progressive people all over the world.30

With due justification, their propaganda credits socialist states for the popularity of certain important para-legal concepts of collective rights: the struggle against apartheid and racial discrimination, the right to self-determination of the peoples in European colonies; the constitutional-legal emancipation of women. To justify such claims, the socialist bloc often calls attention to such things as their support for Resolution 2906 XXVII of October 19, 1972, which laid down the date (December 10, 1972) of an anti-racism decade; and Resolution 2919 XXVII of November 15, 1972, which stipulates that on December 10, 1973, a decade of struggle against racism and racial discrimination be introduced. They can also be credited with supporting Resolution 2921 of November 15, 1972 and Resolution 3025 (XXVII) of December 18, 1972, which asked all nations to join in ratifying the Convention on the Elimination of All Forms of Racial Discrimination and the 27th meeting of the General Assembly which dealt with a draft resolution on the elimination and punishment of the crime of apartheid.31 The U.S. and NATO states abstained from voting on the latter resolution, which was passed by the Assembly in Resolution 2922 (XXVII) of November 15, 1972. Resolution 2955 (XXVII) of December 12, 1972, dealing with the right of peoples to self-determination and independence from colonial oppression, can also be characterized by the socialist support it received. Resolution 3010 (XXVII) of December 18, 1972, the proclamation of an international year for women, had its origin in an initiative of the socialist countries.

Just as the U.S. and western bloc propaganda in the United Nations calls attention to the U.S.S.R.'s compromising of civil and political human rights on behalf of collective rights, the socialist propaganda views the U.S. and the western bloc as violators of economic, social and collective human rights. It is obvious that there is a large gap between what both socialist and western countries preach about human rights in the United Nations and what they practice,[32] and it is certain that neither is willing to be bound by all the points in the International Bill of Rights.[33] However, power politics demands that each counters the propaganda of the other in its search for dominant influence over the subjects of international law and the United Nations.

It is within the context of American awareness that, for all practical purposes, the U.S. and the western bloc have lost their automatic political sway over important human rights law-determining organs of the United Nations, that President Carter's new emphasis on human rights in American foreign policy occurred. The utility of this policy as an instrument for the American and western world's retention of leadership in the international arena depended, first, upon its credibility. Having failed to meet the test of international credibility, the Reagan administration turned to a policy of belittling the importance of the U.N., withdrawing from participation when U.N. agencies do not play by U.S. rules, and generally attempting to penalize states which voted against U.S. policy.

In this book, we shall demonstrate that the credibility of the U.S. human rights foreign policy failed to a significant degree because of the U.S. unwillingness to alter its view of collective rights as that view concerns the black and other national minorities in the U.S., to conform with the world view presented in the principles of international law. We will analyze and compare the United States view of collective rights as it concerns national minorities (USVCR) with the international law view of collective rights as it concerns minorities (ILVCR)[34] and show how the difference between the USVCR and the ILVCR acted to impede the credibility of the U.S. human rights foreign policy in general, and the development of solutions to the problem of the black American minority in particular.

The significance of the USVCR as an example for international organizations, for social scientists, for other states, and indeed for international human rights law itself, cannot be overemphasized. There exists already substantial scholarly opinion[35] to the effect that the USVCR does not provide a satisfactory formulation of, or solution to, the minority questions that threaten peace all over the world. As Professor Kelly noted:

> Yet the chances for more meaningful international responses to the needs of (national) minorities are increasing. One reason for the multilateral inaction has been the ideology of assimilation propounded in the United Nations by the U.S.. This factor is necessarily diminished as the U.S. hegemony in the United Nations declines. Moreover, the doctrine of assimilation evidenced by the separatist movement and strong activism by many black Americans, Indians, Chicanos, Puerto-Ricans and others, and the philosophical support minority group rights have received from diverse sections of the society.36

It is important to note that Professor Kelly infers that integration/ assimilation means non-recognition of the existence of the minority.

In his book, *Les nègres blancs d'Amérique*,37 Pierre Vallières, a French Canadian, indirectly accuses the Canadian government of wanting to copy the U.S. view of collective rights as it concerns national minorities. He offered an analysis of the effect of this concept on the black minority in the U.S. and suggested that if applied in Canada, it would have the same exploitative and destructive effects on the chief Canadian national minority. Basically, his analysis was economic and cultural; he saw the USVCR as an effort to economically and socially exploit and culturally destroy its national minority. Even the U.S.'s closest ally, the British government, in seeking solution to its northern Irish, Welsh and Scottish minority problems, looked towards countries like Belgium and Switzerland for models rather than to the U.S..38

In view of the important role the U.S. plays in international affairs and the fact that many scholars have a negative view of the USVCR, scholars of international human rights law and minority problems should be anxious to focus on the significance of U.S. human rights foreign policy in the context of its example for minority problem solving.

The U.S. Human Rights Foreign Policy Initiatives Against the U.S.S.R.

By introducing human rights into U.S. foreign policy, the President has called attention to the U.S. domestic civil rights model as an example to other nations.39 A former U.S. Ambassador to the United Nations, Andrew Young, issued a statement calling attention to the domestic influence on human rights foreign policy;40 he referred to the internationalization of the U.S. civil rights movement. This notion is of importance to scholars of minority problems for several reasons. First, the new U.S. human rights concept advocated in U.S. foreign policy suffered from the same lack of emphasis on collective rights in relation to minorities as it did during the founding of the United nations.[41] Secondly, the U.S. does tend to influence what other nations and international organizations do.[42] And thirdly, the USVCR may not be in the best interest of international minority protection.[43]

The second suggestion was discussed earlier in this section; the third will be thoroughly explored in Part Two. Thus, at this point, we need emphasize only the first suggestion, that the Carter/Reagan U.S. human rights initiative is the same as the old U.S. human rights emphasis, which was promoted by the U.S. during the period of African enslavement and the acquisition by conquest of Indian land to promote European settlement. This is particularly true in relation to national minorities. As we have said, the old U.S. human rights foreign policy emphasized civil and political rights: the rights to freedom of movement and residence within a country, and to leave and return to it, the freedom of thought, opinion and expression, the right to a fair trial, the right to property, etc..[44] In order to obtain the emphasis of the new U.S. human rights initiative, we surveyed, on a daily basis during one year (1977) the following newspapers for articles on the new initiative under President Carter's administration: *Le Devoir, the N.Y. Times,* and the Cornell University *Daily Journal.* Afterwards, we regrouped our articles in relation to the type of human rights emphasized in the U.S. foreign policy. After counting each group of articles, we found that the new U.S. human rights foreign policy initiative by the Carter administration stressed first, the rights to freedom of thought, opinion and expression, and secondly, the right to leave and return to one's country and the right to a fair trial without torture. None of the economic, social or political rights necessary to make the former rights effective for national minorities was ever mentioned.

We also observed that over 50% of the articles surveyed during the first year of the new U.S. initiative dealt with charges of human rights violations in socialist countries. While such an empirical study may be extended to show many interesting points, for the purposes of this section we found, for all practical purposes, the emphasis of the present U.S. human rights initiative is the same as the old.[45]

In this research, we suggest that a successful new initiative capable of competing with the collective rights emphasis of the U.S.S.R. will require some domestic changes in the U.S. emphasis, as well as her willingness to ratify the major human rights treaties.

Thus, we have situated ourselves at the eye of the hurricane by proposing that, if the U.S. is to achieve Senate ratification of the major human rights treaties and thereby a credible human rights foreign policy, it must of course accept the consequences of the principles of international law as they would apply to the black and other national minorities in the U.S.. To deal with this proposal, we must now clarify our definition of national minority, and then establish what are the legal principles of international law in relation to national minorities.

The National Minority Emphasis

U.N. Secretary-General Hammarskjold, in his recommendation to governments concerning the application of special measures for the protection of minorities, stated: "The term minority includes only those non-dominant groups in a population which possess and wish to preserve stable ethnic, religious or linguistic traditions or characteristics markedly different from those of the rest of the population".[46] After a study of all U.N. documents dealing with the definition and classification of minorities,[47] this researcher decided that all types of minorities discussed can be classified under the general terms: national minorities, immigrant minorities and subgroup minorities. We also felt it appropriate for international minority protection to focus on national minorities[48] because most of the treaties and state practices from which the ILVCR is abstracted were concerned with these types of minorities, and because these are the types of minority most often oppressed and thus involved in violent conflicts posing problems for international peace, security and world development.

A national minority, as emphasized in this research, is a minority which was present at the coming into existence of a nation-state, and whose presence usually played a significant role in the creating of that state. Examples: French Canadians, Lapps in Sweden, Flemish in Belgium, Irish in Great Britain, Ibos in Nigeria, Muslims in Lebanon. Other types of minorities considered by the Sub-Commission for the purpose of international protection are:

Immigrant Minorities

As noted by some members of the Sub-Commission, they are minorities which freely and in good faith immigrated, usually as individuals expressing the desire to become naturalized citizens of the nation-state concerned, and to integrate and/or assimilate into the dominant socio-political and cultural mainstream. Examples: Italians in Canada, Americans in England, Poles in the United States, English in France.

Subgroup minorities

They were also often discussed in the Sub-Commission[49] and even at present all possible categories of this type have not been defined.[50] Subgroup minorities refer to segments of the dominant ethnic group which, while identifying totally with the dominant ethny, possess certain differences in belief and orientation. The opinion of some members of the Sub-Commission was that the regular body of human rights law *already provides* protection for this category. Examples: the hippies in the United States, the Dowa in Japan, homosexuals, the poor.

The focus on national minorities such as the black minority in the U.S. is useful because it permits for distinctions that would allow the social scientist and/or international institution to focus attention on the type of ethnic, linguistic or cultural groups that have traditionally most desired and needed international protection. Not only does this focus reflect the spirit of U.N.Secretary-General Hammarsjold's recommendation, but it is also essential to the real political necessity of devising means to stop the development of domestic colonialism and to solve the minority conflicts that threaten international development, peace and security. As suggested earlier, all major minority rights-related world conflicts involved national minorities: French Canadians, Christian and Muslim Lebanese, Chicanos, Eskimos, blacks in the U.S., Puerto Ricans and American Indians in the U.S., the Irish Catholics in Northern Ireland, the Ibos in Nigeria, the Chinese in Malaysia, the Turks in Cyprus, the Asians in Uganda, the Basques in Spain, the Sikhs in India, the Palestinians in Israel, etc.. The history of minority conflict suggests that immigrant and subgroup minorities seeing themselves acting as individuals in relation to the state tend to be mostly content with acquiring individual civil and political human rights (such as those emphasized in the U.S., generally considered a nation of immigrant minorities), while national minorities in the U.S. or elsewhere have often made the type of demands such as affirmative action demands of the black minority in the U.S., that solicit what traditionally we call minority rights.

The Black Minority in the U.S.

By international definition, then, the black minority in the U.S. is considered a national minority. It is also the chief minority in the U.S., the word minority in the U.S. having become almost synonymous, in the minds of Americans, with the black minority. Yet the relationship of black minority demands for collective or minority rights to the U.S. human rights foreign policy and consequently to the international concept of human rights itself has thus far received little attention from western scholars. The controversy surrounding the political identity and status of the black minority in the U.S. remains far from being resolved;[51] in recognition of this fact, the U.N. Sub-Commission recently classified this minority as one qualified for international minority protection. Concerning the distinctness of the black American minority and its general plight, Professor Derrick Bell of Harvard Law School writes:

> Centuries of struggle and exclusion have granted to some blacks a view of life and something of themselves that is valuable, unique, and highly humanistic. The vision contains much that is bitter for the exploitation of labor and lives that began in slavery still continues. Today even the culturally-related products of the black lifestyle: language, dance, music, dress, etc. are borrowed and unhesitatingly converted to serve (Anglo-American) controlled commercial interest as if black Americans, among other services, had been born to provide these needs...[52]

In this research, we hope to call attention to the possible influences the chief U.S. minority problem may have on the American concept of human rights, and in consequence on the concepts of other countries and organizations. Thus in this book, when we speak of non-American minorities, we will be speaking of national minorities in various countries; when we speak of American, we will be chiefly concerned with the black national minority in the United States. Most important, we will analyze and compare the USVCR as it relates to this national minority with the ILVCR as it relates to national minorities.[53]

The International Law Concept of Collective Rights in Relation to Minorities

If one looks for a general legal principle of international human rights law that exhibited all of the following characteristics: first, it must be a general and fundamental legal principle concerning collective rights in relation to minorities, providing minorities with an international legal personality and/or a political existence; and secondly, it should be almost universally accepted as a legal principle of international human rights law,[54] and of course totally relevant to the proposition presented in this book,[55] this search could end at no other point except Article 27 of the Covenant on Civil and Political

Rights, which also meets the three requirements mentioned above. Article 27 states:

> In those states in which ethnic, religious or linguistic minorities exist, persons belonging to such minorities shall not be denied the right, in community with the other members of their group, to enjoy their own culture, to profess and practice their own religion, or to use their own language.

This research will show that the implementation of Article 27 would impose on governments two basic requirements:

* the necessity of officially recognizing the legal and political existence of national minorities (blacks, Indians and Chicanos in the U.S.) living within their borders; and

* the acceptance of the concept of 'special measures'[56] or affirmative action designed to make available the circumstances, finances, technology, etc. required to enable the minority to reach equality with the majority, maintain its cultural and ethnic identity, if desired, while sharing a political, economic and social equal-status relationship with the majority.

In turn, we shall demonstrate that the above two requirements, when applied by a government, amount to a minimum policy of pluralism and/or integration[57] and to assimilation if we omit the right of the minority to maintain its cultural and ethnic identity. Article 27, however, does not refer to a right to political independence. Indeed, the right to political independence is seen as a last resort if the state refuses equality through affirmative action, and is more related to Article 1, the right to self-determination. As a matter of interest, as the process of decolonization is almost complete, the right to self-determination will become more associated with minorities in domestic exploitative situations. This point was stressed by Professor Cahier at the 1985 session of the Hague Academy of International Law.

Having reached this conclusion, we may now more precisely restate the principal proposition of this research. If the U.S. is to achieve Senate ratification of the major human rights treaties,[58] and thereby add credibility to its human rights foreign policy, it must be willing to accept the principles and political implications of Article 27 as it applies to the black and other national minorities in the United States.

Methodology

In order to best explain the techniques employed in this research, we have restated our chief points as follows:

* Given that the U.S. human rights foreign policy claims to promote all major aspects of international human rights law[59]
* Then the credibility and legitimacy of this policy[60] will depend on the ability of the U.S. to promote those aspects of human rights law which concern the chief U.S. human rights problems[61] as well as those aspects which chiefly concern the problems of other countries.[62]
* Also given: the collective rights legal principles represented in Article 27 of the Covenant are important aspects of international human rights law which concern the chief human rights problems of the U.S.
* Article 27 calls upon states defined as multi-national to follow a policy that recognizes the existence of their minorities and provides for their equal status survival as defined by the international law-determining agencies.[63]
* The U.S. is generally known in the world and is defined as a multi-national state by the Sub-Commission of the United Nations. Therefore the credibility and legitimacy of the U.S. human rights foreign policy depends on its ability to ratify the major human rights treaties and recognize the principles of Article 27 as they relate to the chief U.S. human rights problems, as well as those principles which relate chiefly to the problems of other countries.

In order to organize the support for the principal points made in this book, we have divided our argument into its three major sub-hypotheses:

1. Article 27 is the most universally accepted basic and general principle of collective rights for minorities in international human rights law. Its legal principles uphold the necessity for multi-national states to legally recognize the existence of national minorities within their borders and to accept the right of national minorities to affirmative action or 'special measures'.

2. The U.S. concept of collective rights in relation to the black minority in the U.S. and other national minorities runs contrary to the legal principles of international human rights law as far as minority recognition and special measures are concerned.

3. The fact that the USVCR is contrary to that of the ILVCR is a

significant factor in the Senate non-ratification of the major human rights treaties. Both this contrariness of the USVCR and Senate non-ratification act to damage the credibility and legitimacy of the U.S. human rights foreign policy by raising doubts as to whether the U.S. is willing to promote and abide by human rights law by applying those principles of international human rights law which may concern its own violations, as well as those which concern the problems of other nations.

The inductive or traditional approach to the study of subjects in international law[64] is the central technique used to determine what the legal principles of collective rights in international human rights law are, and to guide our efforts in proving the three components of the chief hypothesis.

We hope that, apart from proving our hypothesis, this book will highlight the most unique aspects of the U.S. view and suggest the possible existence of a link between the unique aspect of the U.S. minority problem amounting to domestic colonialism, and the larger question of international protection of minority rights in other countries; this larger question may be affected by human rights in U.S. foreign policy, acting under the influence and restraints of its domestic minority problems or policy.

It should equally be remembered that the USVCR in relation to national minorities is only one of hundreds of other domestic and international factors that influence its domestic and international human rights policy in various ways, such as the requirements of international capitalism, the demands of power politics, the traditional isolationist sentiments in the U.S., the historically powerless position of national minorities, the desire of Americans to identify the goals of their country more closely with capitalist ideals following the aftershock of the Vietnam War, Watergate, Iran and Lebanon; the unwillingness of the U.S. to amend her Constitution to provide for its obligations under the United Nations Charter and covenants, etc.; the economic, political, military and security requirements of a major power; the past failures of U.S. economic and political policy in Asia and Latin America;[65] the ideological struggle between the socialist and capitalist blocs -- to name a few. This book, in singling out the U.S. minority problem or policy, does not attempt to ignore or downplay the importance of the other influences, but instead simply sorts out from this mass of determinants, one which may otherwise be overlooked, one which is of particular interest to a policy of human rights, and one which is of utmost importance to those in the business of attempting to find ways in which minorities in nation-states can be adequately protected, particularly against the possibility of domestic colonialism. This is important because we believe that adequate international protection for minorities is necessary for world peace and development, and consequently perhaps, for human survival.[66]

I hope that in calling attention to the minority policy of the U.S., my endeavor will not be viewed by my fellow countrymen (black or white) as being anti-American, but rather as an effort to highlight and indeed promote a solution to one of the most obvious and destructive faults in the system, one which is so destructive and dehumanizing that it calls for a sincere national effort at resolution. It calls for such an effort perhaps at the expense of the system itself.

It is unrealistic to believe that while the European nations of the 19th century were busy carving out a colonial empire in Africa, Asia and Latin America, the Anglo-Americans in the U.S. were not. Indeed, colonialist capitalism was the economic and political ideal of that day, no doubt shared by European thinkers and governments on both sides of the Atlantic and elsewhere. Due to their circumstances and decision to break politically from the mother country, capitalistic colonialism developed in the U.S. in such a manner as to include the conquered or enslaved peoples within the geographic and political entity of the state formed by the conquerors. If not rectified, this results in a state in which national minorities are exploited, dominated and discriminated against. In this book, we refer to this state of affairs as domestic colonialism, a much more subtle form of colonialism than that which was practiced in the Third World and, because it concerns minorities, much more difficult to target, objectify, discuss or eliminate. It is interwoven into the fabric of the national institutions and is identified, rightfully, as an historical aspect of the national political and social culture. However, it is a deadly form of oppression that denies not only the equality of the national minority concerned, but also its right to exist politically and culturally. If not checked, it threatens to transform national minorities into a permanent underclass whose rights only exist when in the interest of the majority, and whose culture, labor and creativity must remain at the disposal of the oppressor for his immediate benefit and enjoyment.

CHAPTER 1

UNITED NATIONS DEFINITION OF
THE TERM "MINORITY"

In order for nation-states to cooperate in ways conceived of as mutually beneficial in a world governed by interdependence and power politics, they were obliged to create the basic principles by which each was expected to abide. Those principles which were universally accepted became the fundamental principles of international law: sovereignty, recognition, consent, good faith, self-defense, international responsibility, freedom of the seas, etc..[67] In our approach to the study of problems concerning international minority rights and indeed international law itself, in the context of power politics, the principle of sovereignty-equality is seen to possess a disproportional importance in relation to the other basic principles. As Professor Schwarzenberger wrote:

In order to understand (the origin of such principles), we must bear in mind the ensemble of the full subjects of international law in a state of sovereign coexistence. If none of them recognizes a common worldly superior, the starting-point for any cooperation amongst them is necessarily that of mutual concession of equality of status (or sovereignty)...[68]

The striking similarity between these fundamental principles including the disproportional importances of sovereignty-equality, and what are often referred to as principles of diplomacy or inter-state relations, points to the obvious interlocked relationship between the discipline of international law and international relations.

In their book, *International Law and the Social Sciences,* Wesley L. Gould and Michael Barkun write:

...With the exception of writers whose sense of 'realism' impels them to argue that law is non-existent in international relations, those individuals who turn their attention to international law hold the conviction that law has something to do with international relations... It must be the case for the practitioner, whether a legal adviser to a Foreign Ministry or a member of a law firm, for otherwise there would be nothing of international scope on which to practice the lawyer's art... Anecdotal support for various optimistic and pessimistic portrayals of law's place in the international scene hardly carries knowledge beyond the limits imposed by acceptance of either the myth of the rule of law, or the myth of the dominance of power... International law has been subjected to the onslaughts of fierce polemical literature, but, strangely, its detractors never deal with life in a hypothetical world without the semblance of international law. Untestable as such a life is in the real world, it is worth examining in the simulated worlds of the imagination. A world constructed in this fashion would be unlikely to remain long in its 'outlaw' state. Law, like Voltaire's deity, would have to be invented.69

A second important aspect of our approach is the realization that power politics places limits on international law. That is, that international law *(lex lata)* is only what states have accepted as legal rules of law, and that any attempt to logically deduce from legal principles rules of law which are not in accordance with what states have been able to accept due to politico-economic processes, amounts to an opinion of what ought to be law.

The significance of these two aspects of our approach are: they tend to eliminate the gap between international law and the real world, by calling for international legal materials to be interpreted so as to permit adequate consideration of the restraints imposed on states by the international system in which they are the principal actors and in the case of international law, the principal subjects. (Thus in this book, we compare the actual USVCR, Part Two, with the actual ILVCR, Part One). We have used the techniques of historical analysis (Part Two) in supporting the principal hypothesis of this book. We suggest the political notion that nations accept principles of and adhere to obligations in international law in order to maintain or improve their position vis-a-vis each other and in the international decision-making organizations. Rightly or wrongly, states feel that the more they associate their objectives with international law (or universally acceptable concepts), the greater will be their influence (power), especially in those international areas that are important to their national interest. In essence, our approach suggests that in international relations, a state must often be willing to accept and fulfill certain relevant legal obligations in order to further its political national interest goals, and that such legal obligations are limited to those which are considered by a significant number of states to be morally and/or legally correct. Thus, in investigating the evolution of both the USVCR and the ILVCR, and the effect of the difference between them, we highlight both legal proceedings and political causation.

In short, our approach suggests, as before mentioned, that not only are the law-creating processes of international law conditioned by the nature of the political arena, but that the political environment also conditions the law-determining processes.

Also important is the realization that terminology in international law often has both legal and political connotations, and the 'rights' associated with terms often have the connotation of political goals. For example, a minority may be a legally-defined group, but without a successful political demand from that group for its collective rights to cultural independence from the majority ethny, the United Nations is often powerless under international law to officially recognize those rights for the group concerned. After a group has demonstrated its capacity to demand a change in its domestic minority status towards cultural independence or some form of self-determination, the terminology in human rights law is sufficiently vague as to permit the national and international political processes to play a significant role in determining the outcome of almost any conceivable demand.

Thus far, we have emphasized the theoretical, empirical and political nature of our approach, but what about the normative legal aspects and how do these aspects tie in with the empirical and political aspects? We have said that the real world of political processes plays a major role in the law creating processes and law interpreting processes of international law, and that for this reason we must empirically as well as logically investigate problems in international law. Now we may ask precisely which processes are nearly universally accepted as legal sources of international law, and which agencies are nearly universally accepted by states as having the legal authority to interpret law? Since we have said that the legally binding rules of international law are to a large measure those which states accept as legally binding, this brings us to the normative and legal aspect of our approach.

Article 38 of the Statute of the World Court, which itself is nearly universally accepted, tells us that there are three primary law creating processes in international law:

1. international conventions
2. international customs
3. the general principles of law recognized by civilized nations.

Professors Schwarzenberger and Keeton affirm that:

...For the purpose of grading the law determining agencies, Article 38 of the Statute distinguishes between principal and subsidiary agencies. The practice of those subjects of international law which are parties to a convention forms a principal agency; for a convention is direct evidence of law accepted by the parties to it.... Consequently, every individual subject of international law is but a component element of a principal agency. In the absence of the direct evidence of conventions and other compound evidence of an international consensus, courts, international and national, as well as the most highly qualified publicists are merely subsidiary means of determining the state of law on a given subject. (See diagram)

The hierarchy of law determining (secondary sources of law) agencies goes from the International Court of Justice at the top, to international tribunals, then national courts, and on down to publicists and finally to the actions and declarations of states. However, since state representatives in international agencies usually vote in accordance with the wishes of their state, it is also politically correct to say that the subjects of international law (the states) are the highest law-determining agencies. As before mentioned, this hierarchy intends to give higher credence to those agencies less likely to be unacceptably influenced or controlled by the political goals of any one state or one set of states.[70]

Article 38 of the Statute embodies two different hierarchies. One, the hierarchy of law creating processes, is established in a straightforward manner; treaties take precedence over international customary law, and international customary law comes before the general principles of law recognized by civilized nations. The other is the hierarchy of agencies which furnish evidence of what are, at a given time, the rules of international law.[71]

This means that the rules of international law may always be viewed as provisional until more evidence or different authoritative interpretations are forthcoming. This is important when we realize that the changing nature of power relations in the international system is likely to call for changes in rules.

Although the complexity of Article 38 of the Statute of the World Court and its interpretations could easily be the subject of a thesis, we feel that we have exposed the essential elements of our approach necessary for understanding the presentation of the material in this book.

The purpose of Part One is to show that the principle embodied in Article 27 of the Covenant on Civil and Political Rights represents the most general and almost universally accepted norms of international law in relation to minorities. However, we do not intend to suggest that this general principle has of yet entered into customary

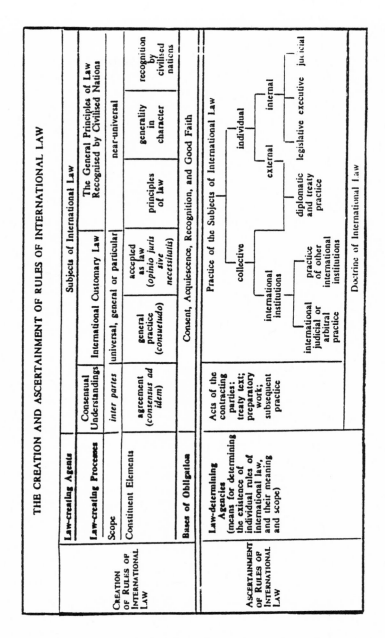

Figure 1: The Creation and Ascertainment of Rules of International Law. Source: Georg Schwarzenberger, *The Inductive Approach to International Law,* Stevens and Sons, London, 1965, p. 20.

international law, or has acquired in any way the status of a rule of law. We simply will suggest that the legal principle exists, and that it is in the process of being accepted by states; that this general principle represented by Article 27 can be abstracted from the practices of states, or seen in treaties and other consensual understandings. We also feel that Article 27, by calling for 'special measures' and recognition of minorities, is presently the fundamental international legal principle regarding collective rights as it concerns national minorities. To support this interpretation of Article 27, we will rely heavily on the most current documents of the only law determining agency to recently deal in detail with the interpretation of this article and to have reached a consensual understanding as to its appropriate interpretation in relation to minorities: the Sub-Commission for the Prevention of Discrimination and Protection of Minorities.72 Wherever possible, we will supplement the interpretation of the Sub-Commission with views from other international organizations, the International Court of Justice, and of course, from the opinions of highly qualified publicists.

Part One is arranged to demonstrate the following:

1. that Article 27 represents the essence of the ILVCR
2. that it is almost universally accepted, and
3. that it contains two chief obligations: recognition and special measures (affirmative action).

It is quite appropriate that we begin the first part of this research by defining the term minority, for although in popular language the meaning of the term may seem self-evident, the United Nations' meaning of this term differs, having both an objective and subjective denotation, and having rights associated with it which may be seen as political goals. The highest organ in the United Nations to have agreed on a definition of the term minority is the Sub-Commission, which only recently submitted its definition to the Commission./3 While the Commission is expected to give its approval, at the time of this writing the Commission was still in the process of studying the Sub-Commission's proposals.74 Thus, as in most non-fundamental international law concepts, the United Nations minority definition remains quite provisional. However, the definition proposed by the Sub-Commission is the most complete and authoritative definition available. Therefore it has served as a guideline for defining minorities in this research.

The General Criterion

In general, ethnic minority refers to categories of the population which distinguish themselves or are distinguished by the majority groups as differing in acquired behavioral characteristics of culture.[75] Ethnic minority may be said to refer to cultural minorities in the broadest sense, and although the terms racial and ethnic have often been used to mean the same, in international law, they are seen as being quite different. One of the first resolutions of the General Assembly (Resolution E/CN.4/Sub.2/103) to recognize the existence of minorities in certain countries used the term racial to refer to ethnic minorities. However, during the Sub-Commission discussion, it was pointed out that the word "ethnic " was more appropriate as it referred to all biological, cultural and historical characteristics, whereas "racial" referred only to inherited physical characteristics.[76] Also, in this connection the 1949 Convention on the Prevention and Punishment of the Crime of Genocide uses the term "ethnic" to cover cultural, physical and historical characteristics of a group.[77]

The distinction between racial and cultural is clarified in U.N. Docs. E/CN.4/Sub.2/SR.48 and E/CN.4/Sub.2/384/Add 2. The former states:

Whereas race is strictly a question of *heredity,* culture is essentially one of *tradition* in the broadest sense, which included the formal training of the young in a body of knowledge or a creed, the inheriting of customs or attitudes from previous generations, the borrowing of techniques or fashions from other countries, the spread of opinions through propaganda or conversation, the adoption - or 'selling' - of new products or devices, or even the circulation of legends or jests by word of mouth.[78]

U.N. Doc. E/CN.4/Sub.2/384/2 states:

As culture then comprehends all that is inherited or transmitted through society, it follows that its individual elements are proportionately diverse. They include not only beliefs, knowledge, sentiments and literature (illiterate peoples often have an immensely rich oral literature), but also the language or other systems of symbols which are their vehicles. Other elements are the rules of kinship, methods of education, forms of government, and all the fashions followed in social relations. Gestures, bodily attitudes and even facial expressions. Such things that are acquired by the community through education or imitation.[79]

Besides the objective cultural minority denotation, another important factor in determining which groups are classified as minorities is the so-called subjective factor. U.N. Doc. E/CN.4/Sub.2/384/Add 1 of June 22, 1977, page 17, explains:

... the so-called 'subjective factor' is in many respects dependent on the political atmosphere, and the cultural and social circumstances prevailing in the individual social communities in which the members of minorities live and work. Historical experience has shown that the 'indifference' of the members of minorities towards their national origin, position and rights are, as a rule, the consequence of the social and other circumstances in which they live.

In societies with prevailing negative attitudes of the 'majority' towards the 'minority', the members of the minorities are fearful that any declaration of one's national, ethnic, cultural and other characteristics might be interpreted as a so-called 'civil disloyalty ' on their part as citizens of the country concerned

Therefore, it would be inappropriate to ascribe too much importance to the need of a 'declaration of desire' by the members of any minority in order to preserve their own national, ethnic, cultural and other features and to manifest their awareness of their affiliation to a particular minority, especially in the case of a minority which has for decades been subjected to the pressures of systematic assimilation and denationalization. (This has been the case of national minorities in the U.S.)

The U.N. Sub-Commission also felt that several other factors should be taken into account in a definition of minority:

(a) the existence among the nationals of many States of separate population groups habitually known as minorities and having ethnic, religious or linguistic traditions or characteristics which differ from those of the rest of the population and which should be protected by special measures at the national and international levels so that they may preserve and develop such traditions or characteristics;

(b) The existence of a special factor, namely, that certain minority groups do not need protection. Such groups include, above all, those which, while numerically smaller than the rest of the population, constitute the dominant element in it and those who seek to be treated in exactly the same way as the rest of the population; (e. whites in South Africa, or Washington, D.C., or Atlanta, etc.) ...

...(d) the risk of taking measures that might lend themselves to misuse among a minority whose members' spontaneous desires might be disturbed by parties interested in fomenting amongst them a disloyalty to the state in which they live. (This means that a minority must first and always attempt to achieve equal-status relations or self-determination within the framework of maintaining the peaceful unity of the States concerned. Only when and if the State fails to provide the means necessary for equal status relations does the minority international protection accept the right of national liberation or self-determination for the minority.)

(e) The undesirability of affording protection to practices which are inconsistent with the rights proclaimed in the Universal Declaration of Human Rights. (Example: racist practices rather than national liberation philosophy).

(f) The difficulties raised by claims to the status of minorities by groups so small that special treatment could, for instance, place a disproportionate burden upon the resources of the State.80 (Example: may affect certain demands of Native Americans)

Under these circumstances and considerations, a minority may be of the following origins:
(a) it may formerly have constituted an independent nation with its own State (or a more or less independent tribal organization). (Example: the Native American)

(b) It may formerly have been part of a nation living under its own State, which was later segregated from this jurisdiction and annexed to another State. (Example: Chicanos in southwestern U.S.) or

(c) It may have been, or may still be, a regional or scattered group which, although bound to the predominant group by certain feelings or solidarity, has not reached even a minimum degree of real assimilation with the predominant group. (Example: the black American minority)

Types of Minorities
The existence of several types of minorities was recognized, although the Sub-Commission and Article 27 emphasize only three general types: linguistic, ethnic and religious groups;81 and no differences in the type of rights accorded to each distinction were mentioned. Since ethnic includes race, all national minorities in the U.S. could be classified under this category. However, in Sub-Commission discussions, other non-official distinctions were drawn between:

"historical", "classical", or "involuntary" minorities, resulting from events of a historical or geographical character (for example, changes in the borders, transfer of population, and slavery) and "minorities by election", "voluntary minorities" or "new minorities" composed of persons who had recently and voluntarily left their country of origin and moved to other countries (such as immigrants and foreign migrant workers).

In relation to the origin of groups and their situation in relation to the State, the following types of minorities were mentioned by the Sub-Commission:

(a) Groups which existed in the country before the establishment of the State. (Example: Chicanos, Africans, Native Americans; these are national minorities)...

...(c) Groups formed by persons having a common origin, religion and language who have become nationals of the State.[82] (Example: Italian, Polish and other immigrants. Their internationally protected rights are limited to civil rights and the right to assimilate, maintain their culture and language, or to return to their homeland.)

Demand for Additional Consideration

Some members of the Sub-Commission indicated that national minorities (as emphasized in this book) should be conceived of as having different needs than sub-group or immigrant minorities (as defined in this book):

Many delegations representing countries of immigration stressed... that persons of similar origin who entered their territories voluntarily, through a gradual process of immigration, could not be regarded as minorities, as this would endanger the national integrity of the receiving States; while the newcomers were free to use their own language and follow their own religion, they were expected to become part of the national fabric.[83]

Another Sub-Commission commentary states:

In historical surveys of the origin and establishment of ethnic, religious and linguistic minorities in the country, it should be indicated in particular whether the presence of these minorities is due to the existence of an autochthonous population, immigration, or an alteration of the country's borders.[84]

Yet another reads:

In this connection it should be added that the sense of identity of minority groups is generally much stronger among groups constituted by people who are a minority, not by their own choice, but because they have been included within the national border of a State by political accident.[85]

Several representatives of Latin American countries maintained that the problem of minorities did not arise in the American continent in the same way as in Europe, and recalled that the Eighth International Conference of American States had approved a resolution stating that immigrants were not entitled to demand special treatment as a community.[86] This position was defended on the grounds that the rights of minorities were not mentioned in the Universal Declaration of Human Rights adopted in 1948 by the General Assembly of the United Nations.

Other governments which accepted the need in general for national and immigrant minority protection, felt it should not be extended to types of immigrant minorities that were not permanent (migratory immigrant minorities). According to such governments, migrant workers should not be considered minorities because they usually did not acquire the citizenship of the State wherein they temporarily established themselves, and consequently they did not enjoy the political rights of citizens. Some states felt that migrant workers represented a new and special category of minority, possibly a "social minority".[87] It was also noted that special problems arose in developing countries, and that the case of tribes should not be confused with that of minorities in the industrialized countries.[88]

Yet other governments, such as that of the U.S.A., which have not explicitly recognized the existence of minorities within their borders, indicated that the objective of their policy is 'cohesion and unity of their people (through assimilation and Anglo-Americanization) and the creation of an atmosphere in which the various ethnic, religious and linguistic groups may find the opportunity to transcend the differences between them', (thus leaving the Anglo-American in the superior position of overseeing this unending process and setting the rules and conditions by which it proceeds). On the basis of that assumption, the tendency of such governments has been to de-emphasize the scope of intergroup differences, or often even to deny their existence altogether.[89] A U.S. argument to this effect is that special measures or affirmative action for minority protection aimed at ensuring equality between the majority and minority, inevitably leads to differences in treatment (since such are necessary to provide the weaker equal status), and that such a situation contains the seeds of reverse discrimination.[90] The response of the Sub-Commission to such arguments can be seen in the conclusions it reached.

Conclusions of the Sub-Commission

After listening to all the arguments, the Sub-Commission reached the following conclusions:

...that while equality and non-discrimination imply a formal guarantee of uniform treatment for all individuals, protection of minorities implies special measures (or affirmative action) in favour of members of a minority group; the purpose of these measures nonetheless is to institute a factual equality between the members of such groups and other individuals. The prevention of discrimination on the one hand and the implementation of special measures to protect minorities, on the other, are merely two aspects of the same problem. The guiding principle is that no individual should be placed at a disadvantage merely because he is a member of a particular minority .91

The Sub-Commission further stated:

From available information, harmonious relations between various ethnic, religious and linguistic groups within a country depend to a large extent on the attitude of the dominant political forces of the society of that country and on their willingness to allow members of each group to pursue their economic, social and cultural development according to their own tradition in an atmosphere free of discrimination (thus implying that if a national minority is forced to develop only according to the traditions of the dominant, eg. Anglo-American, group, not only do we have non-harmonious relations, but also the domination and developmental retardation of the minority.) When population groups are assured of their rights, when they are able to participate fully in the political, economic and social life of their country, when the contributions of their culture (not their contribution to the dominant, eg. Anglo-American, culture) are recognized, they gain the sense of security which is indispensable for the elimination of intergroup tension...

... that intergroup tension and friction may be attributed to a number of causes, including the adoption by States of a policy of forced assimilation, the discriminatory practices to which population groups may be subject, economic imbalance between population groups, differences in outlook between groups, and the stereotyped views held by groups concerning one another. With regard to developing countries, the negative consequences of colonialism are to be added to the list.

The Sub-Commission further concluded that the principles of international law require states to officially recognize the existence of their minorities with the understanding that 'the objective presence of sufficient evidence to indicate that the minority exists is sufficient to make applicable the pertinent international rules, foremost of which is

Article 27 of the Covenant on Civil and Political Rights.' As for the question of implicit recognition, 'general constitutional provisions forbidding discrimination based on race, national or ethnic origin, religion or language cannot be interpreted as constituting a recognition of ethnic, cultural, religious or linguistic minorities'; that most of the objections to the application of Article 27 to all U.N.-defined minorities can be classified under the following headings:

l) risk of interference in the internal affairs of States, 2) the diversity of situation, and 3) the threat to the stability of the State. These objections are basically the same as those raised for many years in respect to international protection of human rights in general ... Furthermore, governments would prefer to have a free hand in the treatment of their minorities. While some states on their own initiative have devised effective protection systems and models, the idea that every State must conform to international standards and a degree of international control encounters great opposition.93

In order to fulfill its mandate to come up with a suitable definition of the term minority, the Sub-Commission approved and submitted the following definition:

...the term 'minority' may be taken to refer to: a group numerically inferior to the rest of the population of a State, in a non-dominant position, whose members, being nationals of the State, possess ethnic, racial, religious or linguistic characteristics differing from those of the rest of the population and show, if only implicitly, a sense of solidarity, directed towards preserving their culture, traditions, religion or language... Extent of the subjective factor involved is the extent to which the desire, whether expressed or not, of the ethnic, religious or linguistic group to preserve its own characteristics, constitutes a factor relevant to the definition of the term 'minority'. Whether the number of persons belonging to the ethnic, religious or linguistic group is relevant depends on whether it is sufficiently numerous for it to be practical for the country concerned to maintain minority institutions...94

Conclusions

This book accepts the Sub-Commission's definition and approach although we feel that each major type of minority may have different types of needs, and that all types may not necessarily require the same type of protection. We realize, however, that for the Sub-Commission to have entertained this notion, it would have been required to come up with a nearly universally-accepted classification of various types of international protection corresponding to a classification of minorities in relation to their needs. Also we have observed that the minority rights principles of international law usually are abstracted from treaties and state practices concerning the type of minorities that we have emphasized, and that the Sub-Commission called attention to the existence of national minorities in its discussions. We feel that our emphasis would be very helpful in permitting the interpretation of Article 27 in accordance with principles that are universally accepted and of course, in accordance with international law.

CHAPTER 2

AN EXAMPLE OF
MINORITY PROTECTION INSTITUTIONS
IN A MODERN WESTERN STATE

Introduction

National minorities were defined in our Introduction as being those minorities which composed part of the population of the state at the time of its actual and official political creation, and which played a significant role in the development of that state. The identity of national minorities is interwoven with the history of the state in which they live. They identify their ethnic group with, and their ethnic group is identified by others as belonging to, the state in which they live. This does not mean that the ethnic group concerned cannot at the same time also identify with an outside cultural center, but that the culture of the ethny concerned is also identified as being an original part of the state in which they live.

National minorities, which are of central interest to this book, were seen as being of the type that often required special constitutional and legal recognition in order to maintain harmonious majority-minority relations, where the problem of creating a national identity and constitution in conformity with their cultural, psychological, economic and political needs seemed reasonable if not crucial; where specific provisions for sharing of national and local political power were often required; and where serious minority-majority conflicts were most likely to occur. These minorities, more often than not, were provided with an appropriate political and cultural identity, and often a significant degree of local autonomy. The United Kingdom, for example, feels that in order to create a stable situation between the national minorities of Northern Ireland, various forms of legislative or constitutional protection must be researched from successful models. The U.S. was not included among them.

Switzerland

Switzerland, a country with three national minorities, is widely admired and cited as an example, although far from perfect, worth emulating by other countries looking for solutions to their own minority-majority conflicts. The institutions which make possible this relatively peaceful integration and coexistence of the three national minorities in the heart of Europe cannot, however, necessarily be adapted to different historical, geographical and social situations, although many of its basic principles for minority protection can.

The census of 1970 showed that Switzerland possessed a total population of 6,270,000 inhabitants, including one million immigrants who are expected to assimilate or to eventually return to their countries of origin. The breakdown of the ethnic population is as follows:

German	64.9 %	French	18.1 %
Italian	11.9%	Romanche	0.8%

The national minority population occupies a number of the 25 cantons, ie., constituent states of the Swiss Confederation, each state enjoying significant autonomy, especially in cultural affairs, which includes linguistic legislative power. Until the first half of the nineteenth century, the separate national minorities were, with few exceptions, to be found in more or less self-contained settlements.[95] The French national minority occupied, and still occupies, the western cantons of Geneva, Vaud and Neuchatel as well as parts of the cantons of Valais, Fribourg and Berne.

The German-speaking or Alemannic majority still occupies the central plateau from the German-French linguistic frontier in Valais, Fribourg and Berne to Switzerland's frontier with Austria, the area from the Alpine watershed to the Lake of Constance and the Rhine, and the German-speaking areas of the cantons of Valais and the Grisons. The Italian national minority is settled in the canton of Ticino and in the valleys of the Grisons. The Romanche-speaking national minority is settled in three regions of the Grisons, where the Romanche community has lived side by side with the German-speaking Swiss. The two linguistic minorities of the Grisons do not therefore form compact linguistic groups. The German Swiss speaks his Swiss-German dialect not only in everyday conversation, but he also has the legal right to use it in many cantonal parliaments, on public occasions, and in church. For the German-speaking Swiss, his dialect is an important ingredient of his Swiss national consciousness.

Switzerland is a modern industrial country, and as in other developed industrial countries, demographic changes are taking place. A movement of population towards the big cities has followed in the wake of economic expansion, and such migration is producing sizable linguistic minorities in the larger cities. In recent years, it has been noted that growing numbers of French-speaking Swiss have taken up residence in Zurich, Berne and Basel. Italian-speaking Swiss from the Ticino and Romanche-speaking Swiss from the Grisons also tend to settle in the larger cities on account of the better opportunities for employment .

In the 13th-15th centuries, each Swiss minority lived in a commune. Each commune enjoyed a great measure of independence. Local autonomy in the weak and loosely-integrated democratic association roughly corresponded to what we now understand by national sovereignty. On its own territory, the commune exercised the sovereign right to enforce its own laws and collect taxes. Increasing interdependence among the communes with respect to trade and commerce prompted people residing along linguistic frontiers to master their neighbor's language, but this did not lead to the official recognition of one language, not even in school. Arriving in a commune from a different language area, a newcomer or immigrant and his family were required to become linguistically and ethnically assimilated. Thus, the modern state of Switzerland emerged as a political entity containing a majority of communes populated by different national minorities, possessing in theory perfect autonomy and a linguistic sovereignty that respected by the central government. The central government then conceded the right to speak one's mother-tongue to people who did not speak German, the language of the majority. This practice was first undertaken many centuries ago. Certain 'subject districts' in Switzerland were ruled by 'governors' before the French Revolution. One such 'subject district' of the German state canton of Berne, was the present canton of Vaud, with a French-speaking population. Vaud was not governed in German, the language of Berne, but in its French mother tongue. The relationship between Uri (German-speaking) north of the Gotthard Pass and its subjects in the Ticino (Italian-speaking) was on a similar basis. This occurred long before the unilingual and nationalistic states of the Americas and Europe were founded and began to enforce unilingual Anglo-Americanization assimilationist politics. The right of national minorities to control over their culture, taxes, and to speak their mother tongue was seen in Switzerland as inseparable from the right to one's civilization and soul.

The Swiss Federal State, created in 1848, declared that the languages of the two chief national minorities of Switzerland, French and Italian, were the national languages of Switzerland (Article 116 of the Swiss Federal Constitution). This meant that the two languages enjoyed equal status with German. However, when Fascism in Italy sought to stamp Romanche as an Italian dialect in the inter-war period, thus deriving an Italian claim to the Italian-speaking and Romanche-speaking area of Switzerland, the Swiss amended Article 116 of the Federal Constitution to read that French, Italian and *Romanche* along with German, were the national languages of Switzerland, whereby the Romanche-speaking area was declared irrevocably a part of Switzerland .

After the war, the Swiss felt it to be too expensive to continue using the language of the Romanche-speaking community of some 50,000 speakers as an official language of the Swiss Confederation. For this reason, today the national minority languages of French and Italian function along with German as official languages. Important orders in council are none the less translated into one of the Romanche sub-dialects, and communication between the Federal Council and its ministerial departments on the one hand and the cantons on the other hand are conducted in the language of the individual canton. Also civil servants are required to master two of the official languages. In the Federal Courts and in the special federal courts (particularly the insurance and military courts) the three official languages are admissible to an equal degree.   In the Swiss army, the language of command is the mother tongue of the men in a given unit, which presupposes that military units are composed of speakers of the same language. When speakers of different languages are grouped together in larger units, orders are translated. The most important rules and regulations must be published in three official languages.

In multilingual cantons two or more languages may be the official languages of the canton. German and French are both languages of the canton in Berne, Fribourg and Valais; German, Italian and Romanche are languages of the canton in the Grisons. In official affairs at cantonal level the languages of the canton enjoy equal status and pass as official languages.

The *"Jura Question"* has become a catchword in connection with a contemporary problem that occasionally causes feelings to run high. The Bernese Constitution lays down that the canton of Berne comprises on the one hand the 'people of the old cantonal section", which is, with the exception of a small area, German-speaking, and which embraces the majority of the cantonal population, and on the other hand, the *"people of the Jura"*, which, apart from one German-speaking valley, is French-speaking. The Jura Movement represents the French national minority efforts to break away from the canton of

Berne and establish a French-speaking canton of Jura. Sociological, historical and economic reasons are cited in justification of such a step. Concerning the significance of this movement, the Swiss government recently has accepted a new political identity for the Jura. The Swiss government is also aware that a minority may feel at a disadvantage compared with the linguistic majority if its geographical situation leads to its being confronted with economic difficulties or obstacles to communications. The national government, in such cases, attempts to remedy the disadvantage suffered by the minority. It might, for example, reduce the fares on passenger and goods transport, assist the establishment of new industry, and, not least important, adopt enlightened cultural policies by granting higher subsidies to state elementary schools, sponsor literature and encourage public cultural activities, as required. Pro Helvetica, the public foundation of the Confederation, is also charged with devoting particular attention to the cultural individuality of the national minorities in the Ticino and Grisons, always doing so in agreement with the authorities of these cantons, which are concerned to maintain their cultural independence. For the Swiss to maintain peaceful coexistence between the majority and its national minorities, the majority must not attempt to abuse its numerical superiority. The majority, in particular, attempts to remain aware of the fact that the four national languages, and with them the four cultures emanating from them, are essential to what is understood by the word Switzerland, as are proportionate or equal minority representation in the central or federal government.

Conclusion

The example presented in this chapter may provide the reader with an insight into what are often considered serious or successful models for minority protection and into the kind of problems posed to nation-states by the existence of minorities within their borders.

CHAPTER 3

MINORITY RIGHTS IN STATE PRACTICE

Introduction

Article 27 of the Covenant of Civil and Political Rights, as we shall see, represents the essence of minority rights in international law. However, before arriving at this conclusion, it is necessary to see how the principle enunciated in Article 27 existed in state practice, long before the general rights of minorities to exist and benefit from special measures were adopted into Article 27 by the United Nations.

Treaty Practice Dealing with Religious Rights of Religious Minorities

During the seventeenth and eighteenth centuries, a number of treaties incorporating clauses relating to the right of religious minorities were concluded between various European countries.[96] Prominent examples are: the treaty of Vienna, signed in 1606 by the King of Hungary and the Prince of Transylvania, which accorded to the protestant minority[97] free exercise of their religion; the treaty of Westphalia, concluded in 1648 between France and the Holy Roman Empire and their respective allies, which granted religious freedom to the Protestants in Germany* on terms of equality with Roman Catholics; the 1660 treaty of Oliva between Sweden and Poland which provided for free exercise of their religion by the Roman Catholics* in the territory of Livonis ceded by Poland to Sweden; the treaty of Nijmegen concluded in 1678 between France and Holland, which guaranteed freedom of worship to the Roman Catholic* minority living in the territories ceded by France to Holland; the treaty of Ryswick of 1697, concluded between the same parties, in which a similar clause was inserted; and the treaty of Paris of 1763 concluded between France, Spain and Great Britain under which Great Britain accorded freedom of worship to Roman Catholics* in the Canadian territories ceded by France.

Beginning with the nineteenth century, nation-states adopted a new approach to the treatment of minorities. Articles designed to protect the civil and political rights of religious minorities appeared in several instruments.

Treaty Practice Dealing with Civil and Political Rights of Religious Minorities

Several nineteenth-century treaties also provided for civil and political rights of religious minorities. Prominent examples follow. The Treaty of Vienna of May 31, 1815, concluded between Austria and the Netherlands, contained special guarantees for the Belgian Catholic minority.* Article 2 of the Treaty provides that "there shall be no change in those articles of the Dutch Constitution which assure to all religious cults equal protection and privileges and guarantee the admissibility of all citizens, whatever be their religious creed, to public offices and dignities." The Final Act of the Congress of Vienna, signed on June 9, 1815 by Austria, France, Great Britain, Portugal, Prussia, Russia and Sweden, contains clauses safeguarding the civil and political rights of religious and other minorities. Article I of the Final Act states: "The Polish subjects* of the High Contracting Parties shall be given institutions which guarantee the preservation of their nationality and which shall assume such political form as each of the governments to which they are subject shall deem appropriate."98

In the Protocol of February 3, 1830, drawn up at the Conference of London and signed by the representatives of France, Great Britain and Russia, freedom of worship for Muslims* was stipulated as one of the conditions for the recognition by the signatory powers of Greek independence.99 Article IX of the treaty of Paris of March 30, 1856, concluded between Austria, France, Great Britain, Prussia, Sardinia and Turkey, recognizes, mainly for the benefit of the Christian inhabitants* of the Turkish Empire, civil and political equality without distinction of religion.100 The treaty of Berlin of July 13, 1878, concluded between Germany, Austria, Hungary, France, Great Britain, Italy, Russia and Turkey, established cultural, religious and civil rights to religious minorities in the newly-created Balkan states*.101 Articles 5 and 44 state:

The difference of religions, creeds and confessions shall not be alleged against any person as a ground for exclusion or incapacity in matters relating to the enjoyment of civil and political rights, admission to public employments, functions and honours, or the exercise of the various professions and industries in any locality whatsoever.

The International Convention of Constantinople of May 24, 1881, concluded between Germany, Austria, Hungary, France, Great Britain, Italy, Russia and Turkey, contains stipulations referring to religious, civil and cultural rights to Muslims* living in the territories returned to Greece. Article 8 states:

Freedom and the outward exercise of worship shall be assured to Mohamme-dans living in the territories ceded to Greece. There shall be no interference with the independence and hierarchical organization of the Mohammedan communities at present existing, or which may be formed, nor with the man-agement of the funds and buildings appertaining to them. No hindrance shall be offered to the relations of such communities with their spiritual chiefs on religious matters. The local (religious) courts shall continue to exercise their functions on purely religious matters.[102]

Treaty Practice Dealing With the Rights of Ethnic and Linguistic Minorities

While the early treaties for minority protection generally were con-cerned with the religious, civil and political rights of religious minorities, later treaties, particularly after the First World War, began to emphasize the needs of ethnic and linguistic minorities for protec-tion. To this point, Professor Claude L. Inis writes:°

Just as medieval rights stemmed from religious freedom, the protection of ethnic minorities was modelled on that of religious minorities. People began by thinking that it was a natural right to have religious beliefs and to practice forms of worship other than those of the majority of the population of the State, and by acknowledging that that right should be protected against the power of the State;   later, the right was assimilated to that of maintaining and developing the ethnic idiosyncrasies of inhabitants whose origin, race, language or culture differed from the origin, race, language or culture of the majority.[103]

The full process of recognizing the political, civil and cultural rights of ethnic and linguistic minorities in international law developed after World War II.

The Treaties of Peace with Bulgaria, Finland, Hungary, Italy, and Romania of February 10, 1947 provide for ethnic and/or linguistic minority protection. The Treaties of Peace with Hungary and Romania prohibit those states from discriminating against national minorities in reference to their property, business, professional or financial inter-ests, status, political or civil rights.[104]

According to the agreement between the Austrian and Italian gov-ernments signed in Paris on September 5, 1946, "German-speaking inhabitants"* of the Bolzano Province, and of neighboring bilingual townships are granted a number of rights, in particular the right to elementary and secondary teaching in their mother tongue, to use of the German and Italian languages in public offices and official documents, as well as in bilingual topographic naming, and the right to re-establish German family names which were Italianized in the preceding years.

The Special Statute contained in the Memorandum of Understanding between the Governments of Italy, the United Kingdom, the United States and Yugoslavia regarding the Free Territory of Trieste, initialled in London on October 5, 1954, laid down that the ethnic character and the unhampered cultural development of the "Yugoslav ethnic group"* in the Italian-administered area and of the "Italian ethnic group" in the Yugoslav-administered area was to be safeguarded. In the Treaty of Osimo between Italy and Yugoslavia, signed in 1976, Article 8 of the Treaty guarantees the ethnic groups'* protection. The Austrian State Treaty, signed at Vienna on May 15, 1955, grants Austrian nationals of the "Slovena* and Croat* minorities" in Carinthia, Burgenland and Styria the same rights on equal terms as all other Austrian nationals*. These rights include cultural rights. Under the Agreement reached between the United Kingdom Government and a delegation from Singapore at the Singapore Constitutional Conference, held in London in March-April 1957, special arrangements were agreed upon to protect the "Malay minority" ethny in Singapore. The Memorandum setting out the agreed foundation for the final settlement of the problem of Cyprus, signed in London on February 19, 1959, contains detailed provisions relating to the cultural and other rights of the Turkish minority* in the Republic of Cyprus. Following negotiations between the Government of Denmark and the Government of the Federal Republic of Germany on the status of the ethnic and linguistic minorities in the provinces situated on either side of their frontiers, the two Governments agreed that such minorities should have the right to maintain particularly their minority language, to establish the necessary institutions including the right of the German* and Danish* minorities to maintain religious and direct cultural relations with their cultural homelands. The Government Declarations of March 19, 1962 concerning Algeria, made by France and Algeria under the cease-fire agreement in Algeria, contain special provisions relating to the protection of the culture and civil and political rights of Algerians of French descent.

Perhaps the most important treaty concerning minority rights to thus far be signed is the *"Conférence sur la sécurité et la coopération en Europe",* Acte final. In this historic document, the world's two major power blocs agreed that the protection of ethnic, religious and linguistic minorities is an important aspect of maintaining world peace and detente. Articles VII and VIII of the Final Act read: "Les Etats participants respectent l'égalité de droits des peuples et leur droit à disposer d'eux-mêmes, en agissant à tout moment conformément aux buts et aux principes de la Charte des Nations Unies et aux normes pertinentes du droit international, y compris celles qui ont traité à l'intégrité territoriale des Etats." Article VIII:I states: "Les Etats participants reconnaissent l'importance universelle des droits de l'homme et des libertés fondamentales, dont le respect est un facteur essentiel de la paix, de la justice et du bien-être nécessaires pour assurer le développement de relations amicales et de la coopération entre eux, comme entre tous les Etats." Article V11:5 tells us: "Ils favorisent et encouragent l'exercice effectif des libertes et droits civil, politiques, économiques, sociaux, culturels et autres qui découlent tous de la dignité inhérente à la personne humaine et qui sont essentiels à son épanouissement libre et intégral." "Dans ce cadre, les Etats participants reconnaissent et respectent la liberté de l'individu de professer et pratiquer, seul ou en commun, une religion ou une conviction en agissant selon les impératifs de la propre conscience" and Article V11:2:3:4 reads: "Les Etats participants sur le territoire desquels existent des minorités nationales respectent le droit des personnes appartenant à ces minorités à l'égalité devant la loi, leur donnent l'entière possibilité de jouir effectivement des droits de l'homme et des libertés fondamentales et, de cette manière, protègent leurs intérèts légitimes dans ce domaine."

Note that the highest proportion of groups subject to these treaties are national minorities. The same will be true in our investigation of the constitutional-legal practices of civilized nations in relation to the ILVCR as expressed in Article 27.

Internal Practices of States

In this section, we have not attempted to discover the real or politico-economic problems of minorities in the countries mentioned. Instead, we felt it most important to present what states themselves reported in order to have the clearest idea of what they are willing to accept as goals or concepts of rights and protections to be internationally accorded to minorities. The ILVCR is evolved in principle from what nations have agreed to practice in relation to minority rights. In a purely political sense, we are dealing with how governments have agreed to define the problem, not with real remedies. As before mentioned, many rules and principles of international law can be viewed as goals; thus, the questions to be asked when reviewing state treaty practices are not only do they provide a remedy but also do they raise the issues in such a way as to ultimately provide solutions. This will be important to note when reading the USVCR. Does it raise issues in such a way as to ultimately provide solutions?

Before presenting the reported practices of nation-states in relation to minorities, we feel it useful to say a few words about the main document from which these reports have been abstracted. This document (E/CN.4/Sub.2/382/Add.1-6) is the most recent document prepared by the United Nations on the subject of minority rights. It is the only such document whose recommendations have been adopted by the Sub-Commission and the United Nations Commission on Human Rights. Besides the above, it is the first United Nations document to stress the need for urgent involvement of the United Nations in the question of minority rights. It is the first United Nations document to clearly connect the question of racial discrimination to the question of minority rights, and to suggest that these objectives are interdependent. In this way, it may be said that this document represents the first tangible evidence of a change in the attitude of the United Nations towards the problem of minorities. The Human Rights Commission during its March 1978 Meeting decided to send copies of this document to all states for their comments and consideration, and also recommended that document E/CN.4/Sub.2/384 be published. This led to the unanimous adoption of Article 27 by the Human Rights Commission and the General Assembly. For the reasons mentioned, we feel that this document should be employed by scholars in obtaining present-day attitudes and interpretations concerning the question of minority rights. In the following presentation of state practices as well as throughout this research, when referring to this document, we have attempted to render its essence and meanings as clear as possible by a systematic reconstitution and re-arrangement of the material composing its six major sections. Also in keeping with the inductive approach explained in the Introduction to Part One, we have attempted to give to United Nations Doc. E/CN.4/Sub.2/384/Addenda, its appropriate authoritative position in the orientation and interpretations found in this section. Here, we must also note that this document represents the first adoption by an international agency since the collapse of the League of Nations, of an interpretation specifically on the question of minority rights. Having underlined the importance we attach to this document, we may now present the country by country report of state practice abstracted essentially from U.N. Doc. E/CN.4/Sub.2/

384/Add.I-6, which shows a wide acceptance of certain norms in relation to minorities. The implied moral obligations, we expect, will lead
to eventual legal acceptance;   thus, the existence of the following
states practice may be considered as evidence that states are in the
process of accepting the legal principle concerning minorities. We will
begin with Sweden.

Sweden

In Sweden, a special government subsidy is granted to Lapp peri-
odicals. Regular programs in Lapp are available in the state-owned
broadcasting and television systems. The Swedish penal code punishes acts which have been defined as "agitation against a national
group". Section 8 of the Swedish penal code reads as follows:

Anyone who publicly or otherwise in a statement or other communication that
is distributed to the public threatens or expresses contempt for a national
group or a particular race, with a particular skin colour, of a particular
national or ethnic origin, or of a particular religion, shall be guilty of agitation
against a national group and liable to imprisonment not exceeding two years
or, if the offense is slight, to a fine.

A Commission on Lapp Affairs was set up by the government in 1970
for the purpose of taking measures in favour of the development of
the language and culture of the Lapp national minority. Its main task is
to examine the various problems confronting the Lapps in Swedish
society. The task of creating a policy for other ethnic and linguistic
minorities has also been entrusted to other Government Commissions.

U.S.S.R.

In the Union of Soviet Socialist Republics, the right of members of
national groups to establish associations financed by government
funds is granted by the constitution itself. Thus all the national
groups in the U.S.S.R. have formed cultural associations with a view
to preserving their national identity, and have been formed into
autonomous republics and areas which permit a proportionate share
of their tax money to return for the development of the national
group, rather than all tax money going into the pockets of the
majority.

Hungary

In Hungary, kindergarten and primary schools teaching minority languages or language teaching groups are established in villages where there are about 15 children of a particular minority.

Also a National Advisory Committee composed of government representatives and members of organizations of the various national minorities groups exists. Their main task is to make studies on the situation of the national groups and to assist in the implementation of the Government's policies towards national minorities. In places where national groups reside, the local city councils have set up nationality committees. By law, the system of education in the Hungarian People's Republic requires that school-age children belonging to national minorities be given facilities for receiving education in their native tongue and that the national groups be provided with a large number of cultural centers throughout the country.

Belgium

In Belgium, documents concerning the investigation and evidence of criminal offenses and taxation are drafted in French in the Walloon* communes and in Flemish* in the Flemish communes. In the communes of greater Brussels, the documents are drafted in French or Flemish according to the language used by the persons concerned or according to the requirements of the case. Also documents are drafted in German in the German-speaking communes* of the jurisdictional cantons of Eupen, Saint-Vith and Malmedy.

Canada

In Canada, the Canadian government reports that French is an official language and the French-speaking national minority receives and organizes their own radio and television service in their language. Also in Canada, systems of syllabics for the languages of the Indian populations are being devised by the Linguistic Section of the Education Division of the Department of Indian Affairs and Northern Development, and plans to grant provincial status to the Indian majority area are being considered, and in princiPlle, it recognizes the rights of Canada's aboriginal peoples to self-determination.

United Kingdom

In the United Kingdom, government assistance for the arts in Wales and Scotland is afforded through two government-recognized bodies: the Welsh* Arts Council and the Scottish* Arts Council. Funds for art, music and drama are allocated by the councils, which also provide grants to amateur societies, particularly for the commissioning of new works. In addition, the British Broadcasting

Corporation broadcasts news, music and church services in Gaellic and Welsh, and the universities in Scotland are giving increasing attention to the study of Scottish history and literature, though the extent varies from university to university. A school of Scottish Studies is attached to the University of Edinburgh. Also consideration is being given to returning the territory of the Irish minority of Northern Ireland to the Republic of Ireland.

Denmark

The Government of Denmark assists its German minority* in maintaining contact with its cultural center in Germany. An official government declaration to this effect states: "The special interest of the German minority cultivating its cultural relations with Germany is recognized." Also the penal code punishes by a fine or imprisonment any person who in public or with the deliberate aim of dissemination to wider circles, makes any statement or announcement which threatens, ridicules or humiliates a group or group of persons because of their race, national extraction, ethnic origin or extraction. In education, the Governments of Denmark have made arrangements to implement minority rights by establishing separate schools, or the creation of separate sections or separate classes in the same school. In a statement of 1955 concerning the rights of the German minority, Denmark pledged that "within the framework of the rules which may at any time apply to the use of the State broadcasting system, reasonable regard shall be paid to that minority."

The Federal Republic of Germany

In the Federal Republic of Germany, an advisory committee for questions concerning the Danish* national minority has been set up in the Federal Ministry of the Interior in order to compensate for the fact that the Danish minority is without representation in the Bundestag since 1961. Under the chairmanship of the Minister of the Interior, the committee is composed of two representatives of each of the three Bundestag parties.

Romania

It has been observed that in Romania "co-inhabiting nationalities" (national minorities) enjoy equal conditions for the creating and circulation of literary works through a wide network of publishing houses and other cultural centers which publish and translate the works of members of those "nationalities". Workers' councils of each national minority have been set up and they foster the artistic and cultural activities of that minority. Under Article 317 of the Romanian penal code, "nationalist-chauvinist propaganda and incitement to national or racial hatred are punishable by rigorous imprisonment for not less than six months and not more than five years." Both the constitution and the penal code contain provisions prohibiting incitement to hatred on the grounds of national origin. The Romanian workers' councils are composed of representatives from the Hungarian*, German*, Serbian* and Ukrainian* minorities. The councils are empowered to take part in the discussions of the main organs of State about the economy, science and culture and about measures relating to the general progress of society. In addition the councils are required to assist State bodies in examining questions of specific interest to the minority concerned and to help in stimulating creative scientific, artistic and literary work in their mother tongue.

Yugoslavia

In Yugoslavia, the federal constitution, the constitutions of the various republics and the municipal statutes contain provisions intended to ensure the right of national minorities to maintain contact with their country of origin. Also the federal governing bodies are so constituted as to permit each minority equal representation in the governing of the country.

U.S.A.

It has been observed that in relation to its chief national minority, the U.S. allows the black minority to form cultural, economic, religious, educational and political associations. However, it does not relate to or recognize the legitimacy of the majority of associations formed outside of the government policy of forced assimilation. There are also predominantly black staffed or controlled newspapers and radio stations,[105] as well as Spanish radio and television stations in areas where there are large numbers of the minorities concerned. The Government also stated that it has appropriated funds for radio broadcasts in Indian languages.[106] Under the Civil Rights Acts of 1957 and 1964, two bodies were established to deal with matters relating to racial minority groups: the U.S. Commission on Civil Rights and the Community Relations Service. The functions of the Commission include the study of legal developments and the appraisal of federal policies relating to equal protection of the law in such areas as education. It has also been authorized to serve as a national clearinghouse for civil rights information. One of the functions of the Community Relations Service is to aid communities in developing plans to improve racial relations and understanding through conferences, publications and technical assistance. As regards the indigenous national minority, four committees within the Congress are primarily concerned with Indian matters. Within the Executive Branch, a Bureau of Indian Affairs has been set up at the Department of the Interior. Another organ, the National Council of Indian Opportunity, which is headed by the Vice-President, serves as an umbrella over all Indian programs.[107] The Reagan Administration reduced the budgets of these programs or eliminated them completely.

The lag in educational achievement among the black population can be said to derive in large measure from the more general problem of Anglo-cultural deprivation since the schools are used as an Anglo-Americanization tool as well as for educational purposes. It has been observed by the Sub-Commission, in regard to the Indian population, that for a long time the federal authorities have not taken into account their ethnic and real educational needs and had indeed contributed to undermining their sense of identity and faith in themselves as a group. Furthermore, the severe disabilities of poverty and disease suffered by Indians (caused by the reservation policy of the U.S. government) makes their education most difficult.

In this connection, the U.S. government reports that it is taking steps to redress the situation. Also discriminatory treatment based on language and cultural differences is seen by the Sub-Commission's report as the main obstacle to equal educational opportunities for the Spanish-speaking national minority in the United States. Exceedingly high drop-out rates, low achievement scores, etc. are their penalty for being unable or unwilling to assimilate into the Anglo-American ethny or accede to the most important philosophical biases of white nationalism. Low participation in higher education attests to the fact that education for the Spanish-speaking minority is generally deficient. Among the practices which are said by the Sub-Commissions' report to limit the ability of the Spanish-speaking groups to progress educationally are the prohibition of the use of Spanish in schools, and the placement of Spanish minority children in "Educable Mentally Retarded" classes, not because they belong there but because they could not speak sufficient English.

To reduce tension among minority groups, the U.S. reports that it has instituted the following general programs:

(I) The establishment of special committees or institutions with a view to ensuring that members of all ethnic groups are in the position to play an active part in the Anglo-American culture of the U.S..

(2) The organization under government auspices, both at the national and at the local level, of increasing contacts between ethnic groups, (an activity which the Sub-Commission has observed, does not of itself reduce ethnic conflict).

(3) The use in schools of new textbooks and teaching materials stressing the history of minority groups.[108]

Constitutional Recognition

In addition to introducing special measures assisting their minorities to maintain their own culture, many states report to have accepted to recognize the existence of minorities in their constitution and establish their legal status. The following are examples.

Belgium

In Belgium, the constitution recognizes the existence of its national minorities and established cultural councils for the French and Flemish cultural communities. These cultural councils, each in its own sphere, decide by decree upon cultural matters, education, co-operation between cultural communities, and the use of language. The law of July 21, 1971 on the powers and proceedings of the cultural councils provides that each cultural council shall have the right of inquiry and the right to receive written petitions.[109] Article 3 of the constitution states that Belgium consists of four linguistic regions: the French region, the Dutch region, the bilingual Brussels-Capital region and the German region.

Each commune in the Kingdom is part of one of these regions. The boundaries of the four regions can be changed or rectified only by the Act adopted by a majority of each linguistic group voting to each of the Chambers of Government, etc.". "Each community has attributes recognized by the Constitution or by laws adopted under the Constitution. [110]

The law provides that the cultural councils for the French, Flemish and German communities may deal with the following questions: defence and promotion of the language concerned; encouragement and training of research workers; fine arts, including the theatre and the cinema; the cultural heritage, museums and other scientific and cultural institutions; libraries, record libraries and other similar services; radio and television; youth policy; continuing education and cultural promotion; physical education, sport and open-air life; leisure activities and tourism. [111]

Switzerland

In Switzerland, the Federal Constitution recognizes that the country comprises four original ethnic and linguistic minorities referred to in the Constitution as linguistic groups and the principle of communal autonomy is recognized for each of these minorities.[112]

Denmark

National minorities in Denmark are officially recognized. The government reported that the German-speaking population which was officially recognized by a governmental declaration, constitutes a group rooted in history and characterized by its bonds of solidarity with the German people and that, for reasons of traditions, the Danish citizens of German extraction feel attached to the German nation and generally wish to have their children educated in a German cultural context.

Finland

In Finland, according to the constitution, the representatives of the Swedish-speaking minority are granted local autonomy, the right to taxation, a court system, and the right to use their own language in Parliament.[113]

Canada

While the Canadian chief original minority is officially recognized, her smaller national minorities, Natives (Indians) and Inuit (Eskimos), enjoy implicit recognition similar to the Native Americans. The French Canadian minority also enjoys provincial autonomy in accordance with the concept of territoriality but which is not guaranteed by the Constitution.[114] Although the Canadian Constitution recognizes the language and religious rights of her chief national minority, it should be noted that the Canadian constitutional recognition of the French Canadian (Québeçois) minority results from a pre-World War I Act (BNA, British North America) of England and that the federal government had done little until the Bilingualism and Biculturalism Commission and the rise of sentiments for political independence among the Quebecois population.[115] Contemporary Meech Lake negotiations on the Constitution, however, tend to ignore the right of Canada's first nations (aboriginal peoples) to self-determination, at the same time that it deals with the question of Quebec's recognition as a distinct French nation or society within Canada.

Yugoslavia

In Yugoslavia, the cultural rights of national minorities are recognized in the Constitution.

Italy

In the Italian Valley of Aosta, the French language is on an equal legal footing with Italian; in the Province of Bolzano, German has the same legal status; and in the area corresponding to the former Territory of Trieste, equal treatment between the Italian and Slovenian languages is legally guaranteed.

Hungary

The Constitution of Hungary guarantees to all national minorities autonomy and the right to preserve and develop their own culture.116

U.S.S.R.

The Constitution of the U.S.S.R. guarantees to its national minorities the right to preserve and develop their own culture. It states that any oppression of national minorities in whatsoever form, any restriction of their rights and the granting or toleration of any national privileges whatsoever, whether direct or indirect, are wholly incompatible with the fundamental laws of the Republic. Also it stipulates that the principles of non-discrimination and equality before the law apply to all persons belonging to national minorities. Under Article 140 of the Soviet Constitution, national minorities in the U.S.S.R. each have an autonomous republic with the legal right to secede from the U.S.S.R.. Laws adopted by the Supreme Soviet of each Soviet Socialist Republic are published in the languages of the people which make up the population of the republic concerned.

Romania

The Romanian Constitution recognizes the existence of its national minorities and states that the co-inhabiting nationalities have the right to use their own language before the courts at all stages of the proceedings.

Conclusion

The generalization of the materials thus far presented may indicate the emergence of a norm in conventional international law (the evolution of the ILVCR out of state and treaty practices) as well as in socialist ideology. First, states have accepted international obligations through conventions in order to prevent conflicts with bordering states and subsequently have assumed legal obligations, at the municipal level, without reference to the international context. However, as we shall see in the next chapter, states are beginning to not only officially recognize the existence of minorities within their borders; and to provide special measures to protect the civil, political and cultural rights of these minorities, but also to accept these measures as moral and legal obligations. As we shall see, these concepts (the essence of the ILVCR) were involved in United Nations practice and were eventually nearly universally accepted in the form of Article 27 of the Covenant on Civil and Political Rights.

CHAPTER 4

MINORITY RIGHTS
IN THE UNITED NATIONS PRACTICE

Historical Perspective

The Charter of the United Nations, in a series of articles, upholds the principles of universal respect for human rights and fundamental freedoms including non-discrimination and equality, all of which are essential elements of minority protection.[117] However, neither the Charter nor the Universal Declaration of Human Rights adopted by the General Assembly on December 10, 1948 contain any reference to the special rights of persons belonging to ethnic, linguistic or religious minorities. As before mentioned, for some representatives, the omission of such a reference considerably limited the scope of the Declaration. Others, more influential states including the U.S., took the view that, considering its complexity, the question warranted further study. Thus, early in 1948, the Assembly rejected a proposal by the representative of the Soviet Union that the following paragraph be included in the Declaration:

Every people and every nationality within a State shall enjoy equal rights. State laws shall not permit any discrimination whatsoever in this regard. National minorities shall be guaranteed the right to use their native language and to possess their own national schools, libraries, museums and other cultural and educational institutions. [118]

However, in resolution 217C (III) of December 19, 1950 entitled "Fate of Minorities", the General Assembly stated that the United Nations must not remain indifferent to the problem of minorities, but added that it was difficult to adopt workable solutions to this 'complex and delicate question'.[119] Two years later, the General Assembly made another general reference to the problem of minorities in resolution 525B (VI) of February 4, 1952. It stated that 'the prevention of discrimination and the protection of minorities were two of the most important branches of the work undertaken by the United Nations'.[120] Also resolution 520F (XVI) of August 3, 1953 of the Economic and Social Council recommended that 'in the preparation of any international treaties, decisions of international organs or other acts which establish new States or new boundary lines between States, special attention should be paid to the protection of any minority which may be created thereby'. Following this declaration, resolution 181 (II) on the future government of Palestine, resolution 289 (IV) on the question of the disposal of the former Italian colonies, resolution 390 (V) on the question of Eritrea, and the Statute of the City of Jerusalem approved by the Trusteeship Council on April 4, 1950, all provide for minority protection. As well, the United Nations prepared several prominent documents on minority protection used in this research,[211] and the Sub-Commission on the Prevention of Discrimination and Protection of Minorities was established. In addition, the Secretary-General organized two seminars in 1965 and 1974 at the invitation of the Yugoslav government, seminars conducted at the world level on the question of the rights of minorities.[122]

Under the Convention on the Prevention and Punishment of the Crime of Genocide, adopted on December 9, 1948, the United Nations defined genocide to include killing members of a minority group, causing serious bodily or mental harm to members of a minority group, deliberately inflicting on the group conditions of life calculated to bring about its physical destruction in whole or in part, imposing measures intended to prevent births within the group, or forcibly transferring children of a minority group to another group.

Under the term of the I.L.O. Convention No. 107 of 1957 concerning indigenous and tribal populations, it was stated that special measures must be adopted for the protection of the institutions, persons, property and labour of the "populations concerned" so long as their social, economic and cultural conditions prevent them from enjoying the benefits of the general laws of the country to which they belong.[123] Simply stated, this population should not be exploited simply because it has a history of exploitation.

In the U.N.E.S.C.O. Convention against Discrimination in Education, adopted on December 14, 1960, the States party to the Convention agree that it is essential to recognize the right of members of minorities to 'carry on their own educational activities, including the maintenance of schools and, depending on the educational policy of each State, the use or the teaching of their own language, provided however that this right is not exercised in a manner which prevents the members of these minorities from understanding the culture and language of the community as a whole and from participating in its activities, or which prejudice national sovereignty'.[124]

The Convention on the Elimination of All Forms of Racial Discrimination was adopted by the United Nations General Assembly in 1965. In Article 5 of this Convention, members of "ethnic minorities" are guaranteed equal treatment in the enjoyment of civil, political, economic, social and cultural rights. And Article 2, paragraph 2, speaks of "special and concrete measures" which 'States Parties shall, when circumstances so warrant, take in the economic, social, cultural and other fields..., to ensure equal status development and protection of certain racial groups or individuals belonging to them, for the purpose of guaranteeing them the complete and equal enjoyment of basic human rights, etc.'.

Adoption of Article 27

Although the United Nations initiated many conferences to discuss and to encourage respect for the ILVCR, it is only the general principle (in Article 27) as a part of the Covenant on Civil and Political Rights, that has received the nearly universal acceptance as a legal principle by the member states of the United Nations. As mentioned earlier, in resolution 217C (III) of 1950, the Assembly had requested the Economic and Social Council to ask the Commission on Human Rights and the Sub-Commission: "To make a thorough study of the problem of minorities, in order that the United Nations may be able to take effective measures[125] for the protection of racial, national, religious or linguistic minorities."[126] During discussion of that request, Mr. Mansani, a member of the Sub-Commission, submitted a draft resolution in which the Secretary-General was asked to circulate to the Sub-Commission a draft convention to be attached to the International Covenant on Human Rights for the protection of the ethnic, religious and linguistic traditions and characteristics of minorities.[127] Following a discussion, a new draft resolution on the inclusion of an article in the draft International Covenant on Human Rights, prepared by a drafting committee and taking into account the comments and suggestions made during the discussion on Mr. Mansani's resolution, was submitted. This new draft resolution called upon the Sub-Committee to state that it was of the opinion that the most effective means of securing the protection of minorities would be the inclusion in the Covenant on Civil and Political Rights of the following article: "Ethnic, religious and linguistic minorities shall not be denied the right to enjoy their own culture, to profess and practice their own religion, or to use their own language." It was later suggested by a member of the Sub-Commission that for legal reasons the word "minorities" should be changed to the phrase "persons belonging to minorities" and that the idea of a group could be maintained by the insertion of the words "in community with the other members of their group" after the words "shall not be denied the right". This suggestion was adopted by the Sub-Commission and the draft resolution, as amended, was adopted by the Sub-Commission by 9 votes to none. This adopted resolution stated:

Having considered the problem of the fate of minorities referred to it by the General Assembly in its resolution 217C (III),

Having adopted, in resolution C of its third session, a definition of minorities for purposes of protection by the United Nations,

Is of the opinion that the most effective means of securing such protection would be the inclusion in the International Covenant on Human Rights of the following articles: Persons belonging to ethnic, religious or linguistic minorities shall not be denied the right, in community with the other members of their group, to enjoy their own culture, to profess and practice their own religion, or to use their own language.

The resolution of the Sub-Commission was sent to the Human Rights Commission and was considered by the Commission during its ninth session in 1953.128 The Commission on Human Rights discussed the question of the inclusion of the article relating to the rights of minorities in the draft Covenant on Civil and Political Rights at its ninth session along with other draft articles proposed during this discussion. The proposal of the Commission representative from the U.S.S.R. read:

The State shall ensure to national minorities the right to use their native tongue and to possess their national schools, libraries, museums and other cultural and educational institutions.

The Commission representative from Uruguay suggested the following addition to the draft article proposed by the Sub-Commission:

Such rights may not be interpreted as entitling any group settled in the territory of a State, particularly under the terms of its immigration laws, to form within that State separate communities which might impair its national unity or its security.

The Commission representative from Yugoslavia felt that:

Every person shall have the right to show freely his membership in an ethnic or linguistic group, to use without hindrance the name of his group, to learn the language of this group and to use it in public or private life, to be taught in this language, as well as the right to cultural development together with other members of his group without being subjected... to any discrimination whatsoever...

The Commission concluded its session by agreeing that it was necessary to insert in the draft International Covenant on Civil and Political Rights a supplementary article ensuring groups, independently of other general rights, the specific right to use their own language, profess and practice their own religion and enjoy their own culture.

The final text adopted by the Commission became Article 25 of the draft International Covenant on Civil and Political Rights. It read: "In those States in which ethnic, religious or linguistic minorities exist, persons belonging to such minorities shall not be denied the right, in community with the other members of their group, to enjoy their own culture, to profess and practice their own religion, or to use their own language."

It was not until 1961-62 that the 1959 ILVCR proposal contained in Article 25 reached the General Assembly. No amendments were submitted. There was general agreement on the basic provision that persons belonging to a minority should not be denied the right, in community with other members of their group, to enjoy their own culture, to profess and practice their own religion, or to use their own language. Indeed, these rights had for decades been recognized and provided for by civilized states. Thus, at its 1496th plenary meeting on December 16,1966, by its resolution 2200A (XXI), the General Assembly unanimously adopted the draft International Covenant on Civil and Political Rights as submitted. Article 25 of the draft Covenant from the Commission became Article 27 of the final text.

Thus, in light of the fact that the general principles of recognition and special measures (the essence of the ILVCR) can be abstracted from treaty and state practices and that these same general principles in most recent times also evolved through U.N. practices into Article 27 of the Covenant on Civil and Political Rights, and have been adopted by the General Assembly of the United Nations, we may now say that Article 27 represents the essence of the ILVCR, the aspects of the ILVCR with which this book is concerned. The fact that Article 27, representing the essence of the international law concept of collective rights as it concerns national minorities is politically feasible and has also been nearly universally accepted by the United Nations, sets it apart from other contending principles of collective rights in relation to minorities, and recommends it for use in this comparative analysis.

The Chief Principles of the ILVCR

Article 27 of the Covenant of Civil and Political Rights has been said to contain two important requirements. According to the Sub-Commission, the ILVCR, as represented in Article 27 of the Covenant on Civil and Political Rights, calls upon states to take the following two steps:

(l) Officially recognize the existence of the minorities living within their borders.[129] This means recognize their right to peoplehood with equal civil rights but as a different people from the majority, that is, a different people with the same nationality.

(2) Provide for affirmative action or special measures where required in order for the minority to maintain its ethnic identity and achieve political, economic and social equality with the majority ethny. (We should note that ratification of the major human rights treaties is encouraged by the United Nations in order that minorities may benefit through domestic law from internationally protected minority rights.[130] The U.S. Senate has not, at this writing, consented even to ratification of the Genocide treaty.)

One of the most important secondary rights that is often discussed in connection with minorities, once they have been so recognized in accordance with the general principle, is the right of self-determination. We feel that this supposed right is so important both to minorities and to an explanation of why many states are unwilling to apply the general principle, that it deserves further discussion in order to provide a fuller understanding of the political implications inherent for states in the general principle which includes recognition and special measures. Thus we will first define the components of the general principle, and afterwards discuss the right of self-determination.

Recognition

From a study of the practices of states, we observed that in accordance with, but not necessarily because of, the general principle, most nations having minorities provide clauses in their constitutions or body of laws to the effect that the state is composed of certain minorities or ethnic groups. This provided the minority with a legal and political identity. We assurned that it is exactly this manner of recognition that is called for by the ILVCR. Such concepts have been historically practiced by states. Article 19 of the Austrian Constitutional Law of December 21, 1867 states:

All the ethnic minorities of the State shall enjoy the same rights and, in particular, have an absolute right to maintain and develop their nationality and their language. All the languages used in the provinces are recognized by the State as having equal rights with regard to education, administration, and public life.

Special Measures

Although the component principle of special measures involves more than does that of recognition, it too can be abstracted from the practices of civilized nations. In essence this principle simply means that, when required in order to achieve the purposes of the general principle, special laws, affirmative action, financial aid and/or particular political institutions should be established for a minority's equal status. As it is assumed that there can be little equality between minority and majority without respect for the general principle, special measures therefore aims at promoting equality between the minority and majority ethnies. However, even with this explanation, the principle of special measures still remains somewhat vague. This is so because its precise definition depends on the specific requirements of the state and minority concerned.

The three traditional types of special measures to which Professor Joseph B. Kelly calls attention in his article "National Minorities in International Law",[131] are frontier revision (similar to that demanded by an organization in the U.S. called the New Republic of Africa), population transfer (similar to that demanded by the Marcus Garvey Back to Africa Movement), and the development of a new autonomous state (similar to that demanded recently by Mr. Louis Farrakhan). However, it would appear that Dr. Kelly's concept of special measures concentrated on the extremes that only become required by the general principle if the state is unable to offer or politically apply less extreme measures of affirmative action to achieve minority equal status.

As explained in Chapter 1, the ILVCR does not accept assimilation of the minority into the culture of the larger ethnic group unless it is the "will of the minority ", and the will of the minority can only be secured through internationally supervised democratic means. Thus, were assimilation to be considered as a special measure, it would not be applicable to multi-national countries such as the U.S. where the government has not officially recognized its minorities or attempted by plebiscite or other democratic means to present alternatives to the development, or to ascertain the will of, the minority in relation to these alternatives. Also Professor Kelly points out with regard to the U.S., should assimilation be chosen, "the only (internationally-legal) solution would be a supervised gradual assimilation of the minority into the larger ethnicity, (similar to that promoted by the NAACP with the idea of U.S. Supreme Court supervision)." However, different from the NAACP vision, it would appear that such supervision, to have a decisive political or internationally-legal significance, would itself require supervision by the United Nations or another appropriately established international organization or tribunal.[133] Such a tribunal or organization would establish guidelines and a timetable that would guarantee against minority exploitation and humiliation under a sham assimilation.

Although Professor Kelly seems to feel that there are only three or four (adding assimilation) types of special measures traditionally used by states, our investigation into the practices of states has uncovered an almost unlimited supply of possibilities. In this connection, we call attention to the types of special measures applied to national minorities such as the Lapps in Sweden, the French and Italian minorities in Switzerland, etc.. We should also point out that, in attempting to find suitable models to apply to the Northern Irish conflict, the United Kingdom surveyed some of the constitutionally-recognized politico-legislative special measures used in other advanced western nations, and made the following observations:

(1) To entrench safeguards for minority rights may require a decision by more than a simple majority before protected rights can be changed or abolished; a "weighted" majority, for instance, more than two-thirds or more than three-quarters of the votes, in place of a simple majority. An example of an entrenched safeguard is the concept of a blocking mechanism which enables a particular minority to prevent, or at least to delay, any national legislation which it considers to be against its vital interests. For example, under the present Belgian Constitution, three-quarters of either the Dutch or the French national minority groups in Parliament can refer back to the Council of Ministers any proposed legislation which they consider harmful to relations between the communities. The two national

minorities have equal representation in the governing council, although Dutch speakers are a majority in the country.

(2) There can be special representation of minority groups in the legislature. There are several forms. In Belgium, Switzerland and other countries a second chamber is designed to give particular weight to distinctive groups. In Belgium, for example, there are separate cultural councils, each comprising all the members of the appropriate group in both Houses of Parliament. Such councils could represent the interests of their particular communities and have a final say in such community matters as education or religious or linguistic questions.

(3) In Switzerland there is a form of direct democracy or plebiscite whereby a substantial body of citizens can cause a referendum to be held on their own proposals for amending the federal constitutions.

(4) The introduction of civil rights legislation aimed at preventing various forms of discrimination or bills of rights which codify the rights and freedom of every individual.

(5) There are two principal ways in which minority participation in a local state government might be achieved: through a ministerial system or an executive committee system. The essence of a ministerial system is that each Department of government has a single political head, and that these heads collectively form an administration which co-ordinates the policy, programs and activities of government as a whole. In Belgium, for example, the Dutch and French minorities are guaranteed equal representation in the Council of Ministers by the Constitution, regardless of their respective strengths in the Belgian parliament. Any such requirement has to be defined in terms of some relatively fixed and identifiable community, a racial group or a religious denomination, etc. rather than a particular party or political organization, whose structures and composition may well change appreciably from time to time.[134]

The possible examples of special measures are endless, because in essence this principle calls for governments to provide their minorities with the same rights as the majority in addition to investigating the minority's situation and instituting any feasible measures which are necessary to promote the survival and equality of that minority with the majority. All component principles of the general principle aim at the survival of the minority in an equal status relationship with the majority.

The requirements for ethnic survival in an equal status relationship, when applied to any given case, such as that of the Irish

Catholic, the French Canadian, the Ibo of Nigeria, the Spanish and black in the U.S., etc., become quite politically complex, particularly when seen as needing some of the less widely accepted existing secondary minority rights. The political right of self-determination, for example, may mean complex political problems for states accepting the ILVCR or general principle.

The Right of Self-Determination

If a minority is recognized as existing under the general principle, then many scholars contend that it as a people has a right to self-determination. But the meaning of the right of "peoples" to "self-determination" as used by many scholars is itself unclear and confusing, even though self-determination is most often defined in terms of political independence. The term "peoples" is often defined as meaning state or nation. Article I of both Human Rights Conventions states that all "peoples" have the right to self-determination.135 If we interpret "peoples" to include recognized national minorities, as some scholars do,136 then of course the right of self-determination may be said to apply to minorities. However the non-intervention clause in several human rights instruments, including the United Nations Charter, raises the question of when this right is to be interpreted in relation to national minorities; as Article 2, paragraph 7 of the Charter states: "Nothing contained in the present Charter shall authorize the United Nations to intervene in matters which are essentially within the domestic jurisdiction of any state or shall require the members to submit such matters to settlement under the present Charter...'137 This article forbids United Nations intervention except in cases falling under the jurisdiction of Chapter VII (action with respect to threats to the peace, breaches of the peace, and acts of aggression). Thus the conventions, covenants and declarations promoting the right to self-determination can only be provoked if, after peacefully attempting to arrange for equal status relations within the context of national unity, the majority ethny fails or refuses to comply, and a crisis with international ramifications results. For example, General Assembly Resolution 1514 (XV) of December 4, 1960 on the right to self-determination, Article 2, states: "All peoples have the right to self-determination; by virtue of that right they freely determine their political status and freely pursue their economic, social and cultural development." However, Article 6 of the same resolution reads: "Any attempt aimed at the partial or total disruption of the national unity and the territorial integrity of a country is incompatible with the purposes and principles of the Charter of the United Nations." The Declaration of the Principles of International Cultural Co-operation (UNESCO) similarly supports this interpretation. Paragraphs 1-3 state: "Each culture has a dignity and value which must be respected and preserved... Every people has the right and duty to develop its culture..." while Article 1 of the same document states: " In their cultural relations, states shall bear in mind the principles of the United Nations. In seeking to achieve international cooperation, they shall respect the sovereign equality of states and shall refrain from intervention in matters which are essentially within the domestic jurisdiction of any states."[138] The key words are "essentially within the domestic jurisdiction". Once a crisis results from the state not following the general principle, the matter is no longer essentially within the domestic jurisdiction because the state has voluntarily subjected or limited its sovereignty under international treaty with the U.N..

It therefore seems that the right of self-determination in relation to national minorities is perhaps so written and juxtaposed with the concept of non-intervention as to permit the political processes to act as the prime determiners or clarifiers of how these laws will be interpreted in relation to any particular case. In other words, if minority "A" demands equal status and nation-state "B" is unable to resolve these demands over time, and if the level of crisis is such as to involve other states "OS" and be considered a threat to the peace,[139] then self-determination for "A" may in fact be promoted by the United Nations. However, the final decision as to whether "A " received the right to self-determination, and the nature of that form,[140] will depend on the results of cost-benefit evaluation made by nation "B" and its relative power in relation to "0S". Thus, one might say that the right of self-determination for minorities is presently dependent, first, on the majority being unwilling or unable to give equal status, and second, on that minority being able and willing to create the political and/or military crisis required to bring about a national and/or international crisis.

Accepting this point of view leads us directly to a political definition of the right of self-determination: the right of a group to create the conditions, by whatever means, that would lead to their self-determination. At present the right of self-determination remains essentially political in that it must be instituted through political action before its legal validity can be evaluated.

We should note that at present the legally enforceable right of self-determination clearly applies only to people living under colonial control, but it applies not to the people themselves but rather to the colonial territory. However, it is expected that this right is becoming applicable to national minorities under the conditions specified in this book. When this occurs, the right of self-determination as it refers to minorities will come to mean anything from voluntary assimilation into the dominant ethny to full political independence. Depending on the circumstances and "will of the minority", the right to self-determination may in certain cases come to be considered the same as affirmative action or special measures but this is not necessarily the rule.[4]

Many legal scholars, however, hold varying views on this right of self-determination. Subrata Roy Chowdhury, Senior Advocate of the Supreme Court of India, writes in relation to colonial territories:

This writer is of the view that, quite apart from the question of the law-creating powers of the Assembly by a series of affirmative resolutions, it would be difficult to deny the legal status of self-determination after October 24, 1970 when the General Assembly passed its celebrated Resolution 2625 (XXV). By this resolution, the Assembly adopted the Declaration on Principles of International Law Concerning Friendly Relations and Co-operation Among States in Accordance with the Charter of the United Nations (which we will refer to as the 1970 Declaration). The importance of the 1970 Declaration lies in the fact that after prolonged efforts between 1964 and 1970 the Special Committee succeeded in producing the document which represents the general agreement of the members of the United Nations. This is to be treated as a subsequent agreement between the parties providing an authoritative interpretation of the rights and obligations under the Charter and the application of its provisions. Accordingly under Article 31(3) (a) of the Vienna Convention of the Law of Treaties, the 1970 Declaration can now be regarded as setting out binding rules.

In his book *From Empire to Nation,* Rupert Emerson voices the minority opinion that self-determination in the U.N. Charter is not only a legal right, but that it also applies to minorities:

The crux of the matter in a plural society is that it is not one people which is determining itself but two or more, and it should not be ignored that the United Nations Charter speaks in the same breath of self-determination and of the equal rights of peoples. If they are actually to be equal, then the subordination of one to another is evidently ruled out. As the international system has been built on the doctrine of equality of states, so likewise nations may assert themselves as separate and ultimate entities which cannot legitimately be subjected to the action of majorities which they regard as alien.

This theory assumes that every group of individuals belonging to a racial, linguistic or religious minority in a particular State can consider itself qualified as a nation, and accordingly, has a rightful claim to separate statehood in legitimate exercise of the right of self-determination.

Although there is much merit in the deductive logic in these arguments, this writer is unable to find sufficient support from the law creating and determining sources to suggest that the right of self-determination for national minorities has become a universally accepted legal principle of international law. Indeed, we feel that this right is legal only in the sense of colonial territories and in relation to minorities, it remains, in our time, basically politically initiated. Such a right strikes at the very core of the present capitalist-oriented politico-economic power structure of the international economic system itself, and thus must remain basically an unpopular political notion held by a definite minority viewpoint, and will remain so until such time as the international system itself may be differently restructured.142

Ved P. Nanda, another Indian scholar, has called attention to the present confused attempt to represent this concept as a rule of law applying to national minorities, and to its deep implications for the future of the international system. He writes:

The legal principles of self-determination carefully outlined in the Charter of the United Nations resolutions have suddenly come under fierce attack, not from the colonial powers, but from neighboring states, themselves beneficiaries of self-determination, with designs on the mini-territories (and minorities included). For example, now, at the very end of the colonial era, it is being asserted that all colonial peoples do not necessarily have the right to self-determination; that the right does not apply, for example, to a transplanted 'settler' population, even one that has been 'settled' for hundreds of years. Nor, it is alleged, does the right apply to a colony which, before the colonial era, was part of a neighboring state. As shall be seen, the new assertions may have broad implications that extend well beyond questions of decolonization and go to the essence of the legitimacy both of states and of their boundaries.

The concept of the right of peoples to self-determination is an almost revolutionary concept of the 20th century. Its political implications for the future of the multi-national states are deep and numerous. We feel that one negative response emanating from the promotion of this right in relation to minorities is the increased reluctance of certain multi-national states in which grave minority problems exist to apply the components of the general principle, the ILVCR as represented by Article 27, in unjustified fear that it will lead to minorities demanding full political independence.

Conclusion

In Part One, we have supported our contention that the principle embodied in Article 27 of the Covenant on Civil and Political Rights is the most basic and universally accepted general principle of international law in relation to national minorities, and therefore can be correctly called the essence of the ILVCR. We have also called attention to the degree to which the ILVCR may be derived from treaty and state practices in relation to national minorities as opposed to immigrant or sub-group minorities, and suggested that the Sub-Commission, in defining a minority for the purpose of international protection, should in future give appropriate consideration to this observation. Using the Sub-Commission definition and our observations, we have emphasized national minorities' needs for international protection through the application of the ILVCR.

We concluded Part One by defining the component rules or the general principle that would be applicable if the ILVCR is ratified by a state. In this connection, we highlighted the component called special measures or affirmative action, and gave specific examples of what the term means. In order to call attention to what we considered to be the chief political implication of implementing the ILVCR, we redefined the right of self-determination as it might some day apply to minorities, and suggested that although this could be seen as anything from assimilation to full independence, states may fear the implementation of the ILVCR would encourage minorities to seek political independence under the guise of demanding the legal right of self-determination. Now that the essence of the ILVCR has been suitably defined, we shall now turn our attention to the USVCR in Part Two: an investigation of the situation of the chief U.S. minority.

PART TWO

THE U.S. CONCEPT OF COLLECTIVE RIGHTS OF MINORITIES: AN HISTORICALLY-EVOLVED PLAN FOR MINORITY EQUALITY OR (DOMESTIC) COLONIALISM?

Introduction

The U.S. has no single, logical, constitutionally-delineated and institutionally-coordinated policy towards its national minorities; neither does it possess specific and permanent governmental commissions established to recognize and plan for minority protection.[143] We believe this lack of a clear cut policy for minority protection resulted objectively and inevitably from the U.S.' economical-historical circumstances and subjectively and paradoxically from its desire to maintain the appearance of implanted Anglo-Saxon ideals including political democracy and human equality, while at the same time accruing the economic benefits of slavery, mass immigration and the conquest of the natural resources of the native Americans. Re-enforcing the observation of a colleague, Professor Andrew Parkins of Harvard writes:

Hartz sees a close connection between the experience of racial minorities (Indians and blacks) in the United States and that of the aborigines in Australia. All have been victims of the egalitarian impulse underlying (Anglo-Saxon) Protestantism, which made it (psychologically) possible to exert dominance over native peoples only by denying their humanity. The slaves and Indians of Latin America were comparatively fortunate, since their oppressors felt no compulsion to concede equality to all humans and hence were not forced to deny the humanity of their subjects.[144]

These contradictions mark the tortured evolution of the USVCR[145] and lead to the necessity of a theoretical point of view that could permit one to ignore the plight of national minorities when speaking about the American ideals of liberty and equality. This notion goes deeper in relation to minorities; it fits conveniently into the capitalist maxim of defining the conditions of the nation only in relation to the conditions of the ruling or middle classes.

However, the U.S. does have national minorities, [146] and minority demands for constitutional and collective human rights, and consequently grave internal problems.[147] The U.S. policy that concerns all U.S. citizens and indirectly concerns minorities and minority protection is based on three vague constitutionally (legally) supported concepts: non-discrimination, integration, and the same civil rights for all U.S. citizens, which is interpreted to mean equality.[148] The concepts of non-discrimination and civil rights are directly connected; civil rights must be available to each American citizen without discrimination. It is this notion which is supposed to provide the support necessary for integration without minority oppression. In essence, the faith in integration amounts simply to faith in the capacities of the U.S. system as is[149] to solve all problems, provided one has access to the machinery of that system. As Derrick Bell, Professor of Law, Harvard University, noted:

Unquestioned belief in the eventual resolution of the country's racial conflicts is an accepted article of American faith. In political terms, there is a national assumption that in several more years (the conservatives) or after the enactment of still more civil rights law (the liberals), remaining obstacles to liberty and justice for all will finally fade away... [150] (This is probably not a requirement of American faith, but of black American faith.)

The essence of Bell's observation can be seen in the statement by U.S. Supreme Court Justice Blackman, made just after the Supreme Court had voted against the only concrete special measure of the U.S. affirmative action minority rights program:

I yield to no one in my earnest hope that the time will come when an 'affirmative action' program is unnecessary and is, in truth, only a relic of the past. I would hope that we could reach this stage within a decade at the most. But the story of *Brown v. Board of Education*, 347 U.S. 483 (1954) decided almost a quarter of a century ago, suggests that that hope is a slim one. At some time, however, beyond any period of what some would claim is only transitional inequality, the United States must and will reach a stage of maturity where action along this line is no longer necessary. Then persons will be regarded as persons, and discrimination of the type we address today will be an ugly feature of history that is instructive but that is behind us. [151]

Both local and national governments in the U.S. have projected integration as a type of panacea for all economic, social, educational and political evils. Forms of civil rights and integration are presented to solve the problems of minority education,[152] to deal with the various economic, social and political problems of Puerto Rico vis-a-vis the U.S.. Civil rights and integration also propose to be a means to solve social problems.[153] Yet a clear-cut comprehensive governmental theory of exactly what it means by integration, how it is to occur, how it is to solve these problems, when it is to occur, and exactly what new type of society is to be produced, are absent from the contents of governmental declarations and the programs of those who construct non-discrimination and integration plans.[154]

Minority groups have apparently taken integration to mean, basically, justice and freedom. Throughout the campaigns of Martin Luther King, Jr. in the U.S., the high ideals of freedom, economic and social justice were the rallying cry. Integration with the addition of the civil rights law was accepted as the method for arriving at all Utopian goals. The words freedom and justice have a special emotive appeal, no doubt due to the 300-year struggle against slavery and apartheid; alone, they produced visions of Utopia. But again, they produced no concrete agreed-upon secondary program of implementation; indeed, it was at times identified with every U.S. minority-oriented policy except slavery, even apartheid, while also being identified with absolute justice. Taking advantage of the emotive appeals attached to these symbolic words by blacks in the U.S., the government has been able to avoid having to deal with any concrete program simply by coming out in favor of integration, non-discrimination, justice and equality .

However, scholars such as Claude Inis, John E. Claydon, and J.B. Kelly have equated the U.S. concept of integration with the concept of forced assimilation at the expense and humiliation of the minority in the terminology of international law.[155] Whether or not this is true, the term assimilation is never publicly used to describe integration projects, which implies that the concept of assimilation might be unpopular or unacceptable. We suggest that if the minority community was officially advised that the government's real solution or intention was acculturation or assimilation over a period of, let's say, 2000 years, with the understanding that the minority is expected to suffer the indignities, humiliation, and exploitation existent while waiting for the possible realization of this policy, many minority elements would probably work to sabotage such a plan. Besides, the notion of the ideal of eventual assimilation ever being approximated in reality, even given the amelioration afforded by time, is questionable. As Derrick Bell notes:

... more recently, persons nonetheless wise seriously suggested that bio-logical assimilation could (in a few centuries) solve the race problem. This gratuitous insult to Blacks was given in the face of facts showing that inter-racial sex and marriage, even with legal barriers removed, does not occur on anything like the random basis that disappearance of Negroid traits would require... Constitutional approval of racial segregation which was rendered obsolete by mid-twentieth century events is now officially condemned; but racial discrimination, shifted but not stilled by a generation's worth of civil rights laws and court decisions, continues to flourish wherever the spur of profit or the fear of loss is present. Contemporary forecasters who believe that serious racial discrimination will somehow fade on its own decrease that very remote possibility as did those early prophets who probably extended slavery by predicting its imminent demise.

On the other hand, if the majority were told that they are actually expected to assimilate with the national minorities within a time span so limited as to give a present-day meaning to the notion, they probably would, being the majority, defeat such a program. The recent backlash against busing, civil rights enforcement and affir-mative action by the Reagan administration supports this notion, having as well caused some immigrant minorities to react in general against what the government calls integration. Since the busing and integration program went ahead in early 1970, there has been a rise in ethnic consciousness in the United States. As Michael Novak points out,[156] one of the factors generating ethnic consciousness among immigrant minorities thought long ago to be assimilated, is that the effort, since the early '70's, to integrate the black minority has brought some immigrant minorities (who often live in the big cities) into closer contact with the culture of the black minority into which they do not want their children to assimilate. They are said to find this culture radically different from the Anglo-American and a greater threat to their survival as Poles, etc..

The fact that the concept of integration remains undefined, assures the participation of the Anglo-American majority since no ele-ments of an undefined plan can be specified in such a way as to oppose any aspect of their immediate or long range dominance or interest, or to bring about a broader sharing of the actual economic and political power, without the conscious desire of that majority to do so, for whatever reason or necessity.

While no logical, concrete program for the realization of minority protection, using such a concept, can be centrally promoted and organized without shocking into political resistance either many of the national minorities or important elements of the majority, the resultant vacuum is clearly in the interest of the majority. As long as American collective rights policies in relation to national minorities are only vaguely defined officially and have no voiced, long-range, concrete objective such as quota systems, etc., which would suggest definite steps to take, the majority may, each time its interest is threatened by minority demands, redefine the interest of the minority in such a way as to suit its own interest or domination. An example par excellence of this can be seen in the history of the state of South Carolina. In order to solicit the assistance of the black Carolinian population, which comprised the majority population of the region until around 1920,[157] the Union Government emphasized the anti-slavery aspects of the Civil War, and its desire to free the enslaved black Carolinians, thus assuring them that fighting on the Union side was in their interest. However, after winning the Civil War and seeing that freedom for black Carolinians meant permitting many southern areas to be under their non-capitalist-oriented political control, the Federal Government shifted its position and removed federal troops from the South, thus removing protection for the newly-freed black Americans to practice their right to vote and hold office.[158] Subsequently the ex-Rebels launched a campaign of terror designed to force the freely-elected Carolinian government out of office and to drive members of the black Carolinian ethny into the North where they served as replacements for immigrant minorities in the lower paying factory jobs, thus providing the ladder by which the early immigrants obtained a significant share of the American pie.

Given no clear-cut, legally-articulated minority policy, the essence of the maxim that majority self-interest will prevail over minority rights is in no danger of becoming antiquated. For three centuries, U.S. domestic and international policies have been based on the assumption that America is fundamentally an Anglo-Saxon controlled nation (similar to settler-dominated Australia, Canada, Rhodesia, South Africa), and that Anglo-American domination over other national minorities or subjected races, particularly blacks, is natural, right and necessary, as well as profitable and satisfying[159] This assumption and basic belief, which represents the essence of ethnocentralism, is an integral part of the unwritten maxims of the American way of life. However, the U.S. commitment to total Anglo-American socio-political and economic domination is no less potent[160] because it is usually unrecognized, frequently unintended and virtually never acknowledged. There is evidence in the past and indication in the present that this Anglo-American drive to assimilate the minorities of North America has resulted and will result in policies, private and public, that have the effect of 'domination' and exploitation of national minorities for generations to come.[161] Thus the fate of certain national minorities trapped in the only historically recognized geographical boundaries of the militarily and economically most powerful and influential state in the world may be even more diabolical than the most gloomy records of colonialism in the Third World, due to the absolute and self-righteous control on all levels of the minorities' day-to-day life made practical by a national policy that does not recognize the existence of such minorities nor their minority rights.[162]

The historical tendency of federal governments to consistently surrender minority collective rights to majority interest, as will be demonstrated in the following chapters, has resulted in the dialectical development of American minority rights decisions in a manner which can only be summarized as cruel, exploitative and pragmatic. Whether there exists even the intention of arriving at a clear-cut, legally and constitutionally substantiated policy for solving the minority problem is questionable. As clearly demonstrated in mathematics, to solve a complex problem, one must first formulate the components of the problem in such a manner as to permit a solution. At the outset, it is necessary to have some meaningful idea of the type or nature of solution one seeks. Here we speak of the necessity to know exactly, in constitutional, legal and political terms, the type of ethnic relationship model one wishes to produce, and to formulate the given factors in one's own reality in such a manner as to be logically related to obtaining that type of model. Thus, for example, the British, in attempting to compromise with the demands of the IRA and to propose future forms of political instruments to solve the Northern Ireland problem, have first reviewed what they consider to be successful examples of multi-ethnic systems in Western Europe. Unfortunately for the British, they have probably waited too long to recognize this national minority and will probably have to surrender to the extreme minority solutions offered by the IRA. The U.S., however, has obviously not seen fit to investigate the real world of relatively successful models to choose from, or the realistic theoretical world of international law.[163] Instead they have chosen to solve the minority problem by Utopian interpretations of non-discrimination, civil rights for all, and forced assimilation.

The reversal of the aforementioned mathematical principles implies that a complex problem can be so formulated as not to permit a solution. This would be particularly true in the case where the nature of the solution sought was unobtainable, given the factors existent. The American viewing of minority protection totally in terms of human goals to be realized only in the future, such as non-discrimination, assimilation and "everybody is the same" equality, represents the reversal of this logic; their proposed solution would depend on factors that cannot be demonstrated to exist anywhere else in the world:

(a) societies where two or more distinct national ethnic groups do not see themselves as different and wanting and needing certain different types of institutions; (this certainly does not exist in the U.S., and there is nothing in international law or the successful practices of western European states to suggest that this should necessarily be the case)

(b) multi-national, multi-racial or multi-ethnic states that are completely integrated into one ethny ("everybody is the same"). The idea itself is contradictory and against the spirit of justice, common sense, and international human rights law.[164]

The goals of non-discrimination based on the advent of assimilation are long-range goals which will depend on a future perfection of human understanding and the resolution of certain economic, political and social problems. To formulate a policy of minority protection ignoring the economic, political and social problems upon which the goal depends is to condemn the minority to the total domination by (and perhaps exploitation by) the majority until such time as the world's economic, political and social systems are appropriately perfected. Such a formulation would very much resemble the Marxist view of religion: a formulation of problem solving which serves as an opiate, impeding the search for a viable solution to minority protection, and in the meanwhile allowing domination, exploitation and oppression free rein to run rampant under the umbrella of national sovereignty, integration and military power. It is a formulation of problem solving which, in the final analysis, amounts to no protection, no just solution, at all.

Focus of Part Two

Since it is impractical to attempt a meaningful historical analysis of all the U.S. national minorities, we have chosen to focus on the black minority as an example, remembering that most U.S. minority problems of the past and present are centered around this minority, and the effort to deal with this minority has most influenced the formulation of the USVCR.

There has always been a strong emphasis on race in expressing the minority problem in the U.S. -- not that race or racism is unimportant, but this obscures the fact that many minority problems concern factors that are not essentially or entirely related to race. American newspapers, for example, are fond of formulating any specific problems arising from majority relationships with this chief U.S. minority (the black Americans) in terms of Black and White; no matter what the actual contents of the particular problems concern, it is discussed in such a manner as to emphasize a general world problem of race relations. In problems such as busing of children from one neighbor-hood to another, and consequently often from one culture to another, economic and social elements of the problem are sacrificed to analyses based on general questions of: should Whites and Blacks go to the same schools; racial hatred flares in south side Boston, etc., instead of questions like: should African history, like Anglo-American history, be a compulsory subject in U.S. schools? The uselessness of the former type of racist emphasis for realistic political evaluations can be imagined if we were to replace the black American minority with a national Spanish minority, such as is often the case in New Mexico, where the same type of resistance occurs, although the majority and minority ethnies may consider themselves of the same race.[165] A racist emphasis focuses all particular problems (that may concern other solvable political, economic and social elements) on the one aspect that is not amenable to adjustment or change: one's race[166]

The racial emphasis in minority problem solving serves as a type of racism by proxy. This tendency has found visible expression among other European settler groups who,in creating the countries of South Africa, Algeria and Rhodesia, emphasized the racial aspects of problems concerning the non-European national minorities {such groups were termed minorities because they were dominated, even though they were more numerous in population} of their countries. This tended to excite racial unity among the different European ethnies composing the White population. In turn, the created white ethny and form of white nationalism was a factor in holding the non-European ethny in a subordinate position.[167] In seeking European support for their policies of ethnic oppression, the South African and other such settler groups formulated their propaganda in black and white terminology: bringing civilization or saving the western capitalist civilization in Africa and Asia, stopping Communism, etc. (Thus far, the political racist philosophy of white nationalism has no appeal outside of to western European peoples). They sought not to solve the problems of ethnic oppression, but to assure widespread western European and American support for policies of domination by the white ethny.

For analytical purposes, we shall divide the minority rights problem of the U.S. chief national minority into four historical periods:

1. 1776/1865 - Slavery period
2. 1868/1895 - Reconstruction period
3. 1895/1960 - Apartheid period
4. 1960/1975 - Contemporary period

From each historical period and cross references, we shall draw out generalizations to be presented as key components of the USVCR.

In concluding, we will survey the USVCR in relation to the international legal principles presented in Article 27 of the Covenant on Civil and Political Rights. We shall comment on the USVCR's differences to the legal principles of international law and isolate its contradictory features.

CHAPTER 1

1776-1865, THE SLAVERY PERIOD

Introduction

Four historical periods, as mentioned in the preceding Introduction, have played the most important role in shaping the USVCR. Of course, these periods overlap in time, and traces of ideas from each period can be found in present day American society. The Ku Klux Klan (KKK), who no longer command significant support in any area of the U.S., as well as the concept that blacks in the U.S. are there for the benefit of the Anglo-American or for exploitation, represent notions from the period of domestic slavery and international colonialism, while the ideas of freedom and integration of the abolitionists, whose work began well back in the period of slavery, were present in the anti-apartheid, black nationalist and civil rights campaign of the 60's and 70's. In his article "Racial Remediation: a Historical Perspective on Current Conditions," Professor Bell Jr. indirectly notes the importance of these four periods in the traditional U.S. history of blacks: "The abolition of slavery, the post-Civil War (constitutional) Amendments and the school desegregation decisions are the major liberating events in Black history."

The period of slavery produced the notion that the chief U.S. national minority had absolutely no official rights, individual or collective, and absolutely no official humanity -- its only purpose for being in the U.S. was to be exploited. This period began with the rise of capitalism among the major European world powers and the search for colonies abroad. In his Introduction to Gerard Chaliand's *Revolution in the Third World,* Immanuel Wallerstein writes:

Every nation or country of Asia or Africa, with the exception of Japan, was subjected to colonial or semi-colonial domination. The formidable expansion of capitalism, creating a world market that in turn brought about the direct or indirect domination of Africa, Asia and Latin America by a few western industrialized nations, found its classic expression in European Colonialism.169

We may add that the Europeans in the U.S. having the same concept and attitude towards the non-European world added to classical colonialism the action of not only conquering but also settling the conquered territory and importing Africans to exploit. This new twist, although seldom mentioned in history books, was nevertheless just as effective and has proved to be more durable and rewarding.

The Slavery Period

In the beginning of the 14th century, Europeans, with their all-persuasive firearms, began searching Africa for gold, salt and other wealth. They claimed land, destroyed old trade routes, and brought manufactured goods which destroyed the market for native products. Carriers of a whole new cultural style, European missionaries often ridiculed native religious and ethical standards, breaking the authority of the chief, clan and family. Disorganized and demoralized, coloni-alized Africans became increasingly vulnerable as a source of cheap labor,[169] not only for the colonial motherland, but also for American settlers who, in the process of conquering the U.S., needed cheap labor as badly if not more so than the mother countries.

By 1492, Columbus had landed in Jamaica, an event for the European world second in importance only to that of European possession of firearms; both factors permitted access to the vast raw materials of the New World. Within decades, the Portuguese, English, French and Spanish added the Americas' tin, silver, sugar, cotton and tobacco to their African holdings of gold, salt, copper and diamonds. Huge ready-made markets awaited all of these products in Europe, so that only one more element was needed in this global marketing scheme to improve trade further: the widespread use of cheap labor.

In 1562, John Hawkins, one of the first Englishmen known to engage in the slave trade, made the first of his three voyages to Africa. There on the Guinea Coast, he captured and enslaved some 300 Africans and, soon afterwards, took possession of five Portu-guese ships laden with another 910 victims to sell them in the West Indies and Brazil. In support of British abolition of slavery, a British House of Commons report of 1807 described the treatment of Africans enslaved on many of these voyages:

"The Africans were chained to each other hand and foot, and stowed so close that they were not allowed above a foot and a half for each in breadth. Thus, rammed together like herrings in a barrel, they contracted putrid and fatal disorders, so that they who came to inspect them in the morning had occasionally to pick dead Africans out of their rows, and to unchain their car-casses from the bodies of their wretched fellow-sufferers to whom they were fastened." (Ingram, *History of Slavery and Serfdom*, London, 1895, p. 152.170)

Thus by the time of their original presentation to the Anglo-American land and other American people, the Africans had already been reduced by barbarous conditions to the category of the sub-human.

By the time slavery had been abolished (1807 in Britain, not until 1865 in the United States), the degradation of Africa was complete. As the noted black American scholar, W.E.B. DuBois, pointed out: "Chieftains representing a thousand years of striving civilizations were decked out in second-hand London top-hats."

While for Africa, slavery meant utter decay and the assignment of her peoples to a sub-human category, for America slavery was to play a major role in her capitalistic development. In the three centuries,1500 to 1800, some 275,000 Africans were captured and transported to the United States *alone,* almost three quarters of these to the four states of South Carolina, North Carolina, Georgia and Virginia.171 Perhaps the greatest tragedy of these Africans lies in the fact that, after being conquered, they were transplanted to a civilization which knew neither their culture nor their religion, placing them, like fish out of water, at a terrible disadvantage. The fact that the new environment was alien to them and that they were slow to adjust to it merely re-enforced their conqueror's self-serving claim that they were inferior. The fact that African culture was unknown to Anglo-Americans re-enforced the self-serving notion that the Africans had no culture.

In mainland North America, there was no legal protection for Africans. They were reduced to the Anglo-American conceptualization of them as beasts of the field over which their proclaimed owners held enormous power. This fact, illustrated amply by advertisements in the local newspapers, helped the development of domestic colonialism by pushing the humanity of Africans behind a veil of misconceptions, prejudice and misunderstanding. A sample advertisement which appeared around 1850 reads:

AFRICANS FOR SALE

An African woman, 24 years of age, and her two children, one eight and the other three years old. Said Africans will be sold separately or together as desired. The woman is a good seamstress. She will be sold low for cash, or exchanged for groceries. For terms, apply to Mattey Blias and Co., 1 Front Levee.

In the Thirteen Colonies, enslaved Africans were allowed a ration of clothing and food. When the self respect and dignity of new slaves was broken, when they were "broken in", they were grouped together in families in separate quarters which were surrounded by small tracts of land on which they raised their own food. Items such as clothing, dried fish, molasses, rum and salt, which they could not easily produce, were issued from the plantation's commissary. Patrol systems authorized all persons to punish Africans who were absent from their plantations without passes. Maryland and North Carolina forbade Africans from owning animals, assuming that one animal could not own another. Mississippi prohibited Africans from trading like freemen, further denying their possibility for human behavior. Under these conditions, the aliens could not develop. Worse still, the death rate was high and the birth rate exceptionally low.[172] As there were no provisions for caring for African newborn, the colonists, true to their concept of the African as a beast, apparently depended upon the importation of new Africans for labor. Cases where even well-educated Africans were enslaved were frequent. In one incident around 1730, an Anglo-American boy saw an enslaved African legally owned by Michael Dento kneel and bow in the direction of Mecca. Knowing nothing about Islamic tradition, the boy threw sand in the slave's eyes, impairing his sight. The enslaved African's habits were investigated. Only then was it established that the enslaved African was an Arabic scholar. Hearing of this, a British army general and philanthropist, James Oglethorpe, paid for the African to be freed, took him to England, and arranged to have him admitted to Cambridge University where he translated Islamic manuscripts.

Though these poor creatures staged thousands of insurrections, their overlords brought them under control by degrees, forcing them to outwardly accept their condition and alien rule, and to turn to indirect means of regaining freedom. The following random examples of these insurrections are taken from John W. Blassingame's *The Slave Cornmunity* and Harvey Wish's "American Slave Insurrections Before 1861."[173] They are important to our research only in the sense that they provide us with a notion of the type of fears and hatred the U.S. slavery period may have placed in the subconscious and conscious minds of the ethnies involved,[174] which thus affected their view of what collective rights minorities should have.[175]

As early as 1687, Africans are known to have struggled violently to overthrow slavery in Northern Neck, Virginia. Aside from the well-known efforts of the African named Nat Turner, an African called Sam, working for Richard Metcalf in Maryland in 1688, was convicted of having 'several times endeavored to promote an insurrection in this colony.' "Sam" was severely beaten and forced to wear a large iron collar around his neck for life, with death the penalty for its removal. In 1691, the African named Mingo, from Middlesex County, Virginia, ravaged plantations in Rappahannock County and, with some companions, appropriated cattle, hogs, guns and other valuables.

In 1711, armed Africans raided Charleston and the Sea Island to the point where a distraught governor amended the African Act to offer a reward of 50 English pounds for the leader, called "Sebastian," who was subsequently captured. In 1712, New York was rocked by the discovery of an African plot to destroy the oppressors living there, and the excitement subsided only when eighteen African freedom fighters were hanged and the others deported or broken on the wheel. In 1720, small uprisings in South Carolina resulted in the execution of three Africans. In 1722, some 200 Africans in Virginia assembled in a church near the Rappahannock River to kill their oppressors but the plot was discovered and they disbanded.

In 1723, Africans planning to burn Boston aroused so much fear that the city took precautions against 'Indians, Africans, servants and other enslaved'. In 1730 there was a plot in Charleston, South Carolina in which Africans were to kill their owners and all other colonists whom they met; instead, their leaders, Gullahs Jack and Posey from the Coast and West Indies, were executed. In the same year an African in Malden, Massachusetts, burned his owner's home. In 1732, a cargo of Africans killed Captain John Major of Portsmouth, New Hampshire, and all his crew. In 1739, Africans and Spaniards plotted to embarrass their English colonists, and some were shot for their trouble or hanged. That same year, more Africans under their leader called "Cato", wandered from place to place near Stono, South Carolina, seizing firearms and burning houses. Later, after killing more than twenty Anglo-Americans, they were overpowered by the militia and their leaders were put to death. To help stop such uprisings, the United States government passed a special act imposing a duty of 50 pounds on new imports from the West Indies and other colonies.

This step did not stop the insurrections. In 1741, African freedom fighters attempted to burn New York City again, to kill colonial over-lords and get possession of their property. Of the more than 100 marauders arrested, 71 were deported, 18 hanged and 13 burned alive. In 1754, two female freedom fighters set fire to the home of their master, C. Croft of Charleston, and were in turn burned alive. In 1890, almost a quarter century after the American Declaration of Independence, 1,000 slaves gathered together under an African freedom fighter called "Gabriel", legally belonging to Thomas Presser of Henrico County, Virginia. Armed with horses, clubs, scythes, homemade bayonets, and a few guns, they met at an agreed-upon rendez-vous outside Richmond. For some unreported reasons, however, the planned attack failed, and Gabriel and fifteen others from the group were hanged months later. Such revolts and/or run-aways were probably continuously occurring up until the end of slavery in 1865.[176]

This period of no official recognition of any human rights for its chief minority has no doubt left an indelible mark on the Anglo-American mentality and on the USVCR. It is important to note that the American government accepted, during this period, the notion that its central national minority could demand only whatever the majority wanted them to have. As enslaved Africans, they existed exclusively to serve the economic interest of the Anglo-American majority. It is also significant that, although the enslaved Africans played a major role in the development of the U.S., officially the U.S. had separated its national identity from that of the Africans, who were officially neither citizens nor human beings.[177] The effects of this early separation may explain the contradictions seen in the writing of many scholars today who, when speaking of the American history and traditions of human rights, find no problem in ignoring the historical treatment of her national minorities. When Jerome J. Shestack and Roberta Cohen in "International Human Rights: a Role for the United States," write: "Indeed, the United States was founded on a commitment to individual rights, a commitment not only enunciated by its founding fathers but also regularly reaffirmed throughout its history...",[178] do they mean that we are not to give consideration to the human rights of the U.S. national minorities when evaluating the historical U.S. human rights record and traditions? Or does this imply that the U.S. national minorities should be considered in the same way that England considered her colony in India when speaking of English traditions? The problem this type of approach poses is that by ignoring the fact that human rights were denied in the past, it threatens to deny such minorities their present and future rights and humanity. Indicative of same, we refer to the Bakke Case, discussed at various points in this research,[179] and to the attitude expressed in 1985 by the Reagan administration, which concluded that the U.S. no longer needs affirmative action -- at the very time it was forced to admit by every indicator that black Americans do not enjoy equality with white or Anglo-Americans.

Conclusion

The USVCR during this period needs no further exploration. It was the view that the black American collectivity should be at the total disposal of the majority interest. Most important, however, is the question of how such a relationship over a period of one hundred years may have sociologically and psychologically conditioned the after-slavery and modern U.S. view. Although the answer to this question is beyond the scope of this study, it begs for research since there are no known examples, since the rise of ethnic awareness in Europe, whereby two ethnic groups starting their relationship as slave and slavemaster, were able to carry through a program of equality and assimilation.[180]

In delivering this dissenting opinion in the Bakke Case, U.S. Supreme Court Chief Justice Marshall summarizes this period in the following statement:

Three hundred and fifty years ago, the Negro (*sic.*: African) was dragged to this country in chains to be sold into slavery. Uprooted from his homeland and thrust into bondage for forced labor, the slave (the African) was deprived of all legal rights. It was unlawful to teach him to read; he could be sold away from his family and friends at the whim of his master; and killing or maiming him was not a crime. The system of slavery brutalized and dehumanized both master and slave.

The denial of human rights was etched into the American colonies' first attempts at establishing self-government. When the colonists determined to seek their independence from England, they drafted a unique document cataloging their grievances against the King and proclaiming as 'self-evident' that 'all men are created equal' and are endowed 'with certain inalienable Rights'. The self-evident truths and the inalienable rights were intended, however, to apply to white (western European) men.[181]

CHAPTER 2

THE PERIODS 1860-1868 AND 1868-1895

Introduction

Similar to the period of slavery, it would be difficult to deny the importance of this period of American history in relation to its influence on the formation of ideas concerning the rights of the chief national minority. The Civil War, fought largely because of a sectional disagreement over the role the chief minority was to play and the methods and techniques of its exploitation, the North feeling in essence that the situation and condition of blacks would render greater profit under Northern capitalist exploitation than under Southern feudal/plantation exploitation, led to the destruction of much of the South. It is also true that this war was concerned with political notions such as federalism vs. confederalism, unity vs. disunity, and behind these political notions, with the differing economic needs of the two regions. The North, capitalist, industrial and in need of cheap labor to provide a margin of upward mobility, encouraged European immigration to meet labor and population demands, while the South, agricultural, aristocratic and feudal was still in need of slave labor to maintain its mode of production.[182] This period brings a change in the majority's notion of the human rights of their chief national minority. It marks the beginning of the process of legally institutionalizing the humanity and rights as individuals of the black minority in the U.S. to participate as citizens in the processes of building the new industrial U.S. society.[183] The abolitionists, who were also assimilationists, felt that the blacks, once free from slavery, would automatically assimilate into or imitate the larger ethnicity.[184] However, this first victory of the abolitionists for assimilation or imitation lasted about 35 years, from approximately 1865 to 1866 and 1868 to 1895; after each period, the Southern area's economic need for a non-official form of minority slave labor was permitted. The first period ended with the advent of the post-Civil War Black Codes,[185] and the second period with the appearance of apartheid in the South, supported by voluntary de facto social and economic seg-regation in the North.[186]

Transitional Period, Stage 1: 1860-1868 (The Civil War)

This period marks the beginning of the transformation of the South from a slavery economy to modern capitalism. At the beginning of the period 1860-1868, anti-slavery sentiments slowly began to be expressed by Anglo-Americans throughout the United States. Many people were genuinely disturbed by the system, and organizations like the Quakers began their moral attacks, saying slavery repressed natural freedom and the dignity of citizenship. These and other early protests also stated that slavery could no longer be justified on the basis of Christianizing 'pagans' since most owners ignored the right of the Africans to be enlightened. Still other abolitionists believed slavery prejudicial to both blacks and Anglo-Americans and to the national interest of a U.S. in the process of economic development. Gradually most religious groups recommended the abolition of slavery throughout the United States. The names of a few well-known abolitionists to arise from the ranks of the oppressed should be mentioned: Sojourner Truth (1792-1883), a woman who crusaded throughout the U.S.; Lunsford Lane (ca. 1857) from Raleigh, North Carolina, who lectured in the northern states; Charles Lenox Remond (1810-1873); Lucretia Mott (1793-1880) who participated in the American Anti-Slavery Society founded in 1833; and Frederick Douglass (1817-1895). Douglass was tall and well built, dignified in appearance, polished in the English language, and middle class Anglo-American in manner. This man was said to have advocated abolition by symbolizing its goal; he showed that enslaved Africans could adopt the Anglo-American culture and thus become acceptable.[187] Essentially, such personalities as these helped to confirm the idea that all black Americans could be assimilated into Anglo-American culture, while they themselves probably believed that the adoption of Anglo-American culture was the only way they would be accepted or could survive in America.[188]

Domestic moral attacks and cultural assimilation were not, however, the major factors which led to the end of slavery. To understand the major factors, one must recall that by the early 19th century, both the American and the international situation had changed. The U.S. no longer had a colonial economy dependent on her trade in raw materials with England. The U.S. was beginning to industrialize, and needed most of all cheap labor for her northern factories. The main domestic reservoir of this labor was the millions of blacks in the southern United States. The movement of black Americans from the South after the war would not only contribute to meeting the economic needs of a rapidly industrializing North, but it would also have the long range political effect of preventing the black Americans from again becoming a politically potent majority in a significant territorial sense in the South.189

On the international level, Britain had abolished slavery in 1807. Most of the other European nations had either officially forbidden their nationals to deal in the slave trade and/or had abolished it as an institution on their territory.190 France had experienced the negative results of slavery in Haiti. Slave revolts and moral consciousness, coupled with the changing economic needs of the growing capitalist classes in Europe and America meant that not only was slavery no longer the most profitable and durable means of utilizing African labor, but that frequent revolts were not amenable to systemic stability and security. Furthermore, the plantation semi-feudal society required by the slave system did not work to maximize economic output and industrial development.191

When the Civil War began, the North enlisted the active support of the black minority against the Southern forces by creating an identity between northern victory and black minority interest. When, therefore, black American refugees from the fighting began flocking to Union camps for protection, the only U.S. government agency or commission specifically and officially designed to deal with problems of black Americans was established. The Freedmen's Bureau was created by Congress on March 3, 1865 as an agency of the War Department. For the duration of the war and one year afterward, the Bureau was supposed to provide black Americans with a special status by assisting them in their transition from slavery to freedom by helping them deal with their former masters, find jobs, acquire food, clothing, medical care and schools. The Bureau was granted custody of all the land confiscated from or abandoned by Southern Confederates, about 800,000 acres of farm land and 5,000 pieces of town property, with the authority to redistribute it among black American (and loyal Anglo-American) refugees, so that they might, by owning land, develop a certain economic independence. The land proviso in the Freedmen's Bureau Act stated that every male citizen in the south, whether freedman or refugee, shall be assigned not more than 40 acres of abandoned or confiscated land at rental for three years and an option to purchase at the end of that time. Located in South Carolina, the Bureau's four most illustrious administrators were Generals U.S. Grant, Howard, Rufus Saxton and John Eaton.

However on May 29th of the same year as the Bureau was created (1865), the new President, Andrew Johnson, passed the Amnesty

Proclamation which restored most of the land to former rebel owners. His Proclamation read:

That the authority of the government of the United States may be restored, and that peace, order and freedom may be established, I, Andrew Johnson, President of the United States, do proclaim and declare that I hereby extend to all those who directly or indirectly participated in the existing rebellions except as hereinafter excepted amnesty and pardon, with restoration of all property, except as to slaves, and except in cases where legal proceedings under the laws of the United States, providing for the confiscation of property of persons engaged in rebellion have been instituted.[192]

As the Bureau's finances depended chiefly upon the lease revenues, fees and taxes of its abandoned property, Johnson's proclamation made it difficult for the Bureau to carry out its original objectives. Many influential people, including northern businessmen, supported Johnson's stand, believing that dealing with capitalistically-oriented southern Anglo-Americans was the best way to get business moving again in the South. This proclamation meant, therefore, that the special collective economic rights accorded to the chief U.S. national minority by the Bureau as a redress for slavery and as a reward for their assistance in the Civil War were rescinded the moment they no longer coincided with what was conceived of as majority interest.

Soon Johnson restored all the land not already sold by the Direct Tax Commission to ex-rebels who took the oath of allegiance to the President and paid the tax. But under U.S. General Sherman's field order, many black Americans had already moved onto or were still living on some of the land to be returned to ex-rebels, and some reacted by defending their new land.[193] Realizing that the federal government was more interested in getting business moving again than in helping them achieve equal economic status, black Americans began using the same supply of arms which they had acquired while fighting as Union troops. The *Garrison's Liberator*, published in Charleston, reported the following in its December 1865 issue:

On Edisto Island, the black Americans, incensed at the restoration of land to their former owners, refuse to enter into contracts with them. Many of the plantations are, therefore, offered for rent at reasonable rates. Brevet Brigadier-General Buche has recently been sent to the Island to prevent disturbances, and has issued an order forbidding all persons from visiting the Island without proper passes, and offering a guard from the head-quarters to former owners who desire to attempt overtures to their workmen.194

Finally, Congress reacted with pragmatism to the unavoidable demands of the black American minority. It interceded to extend the life of the Freedmen's Bureau for another year, and to confirm the early sales made to a few black Americans around Port Royal, South Carolina, where black American resistance had been strong. Those who had been given leases on confiscated lands were granted full ownership; the 38,000 acres of U.S. tax lands held in the area were ordered to be sold at $1.50 an acre to black Americans holding land under Sherman's field order, and what lands remaining were ordered to be sold to black Americans who had held land but were dispossessed by the return of their former owners. In addition, black Americans not already in possession of land but claiming land under Sherman's order were to be given a six year lease on 20 acres of government land in South Carolina, after which they could buy land at $1.50 an acre. It was probably these concessions to a few blacks, leaving the masses without any compensation for enslavement, that served, along with the ascent of the house blacks, as the early economic basis for the formation of the black bourgeoisie and "negro" leadership establishment.

It would seem, then, that at this historical point, the U.S. was able and willing to overlook any concessions to collective rights in relation to its chief minority, given to meet the demands of the Civil War, that interfered with the majority interest as defined by the U.S. (Anglo-American ruling classes) if these rights were not effectively demanded by the masses of the black American minority.195 To avoid a confrontation with minority demands, the government made apparent concessions which had the effect in practice of stabilizing the post Civil War domestic environment and returning it to business as usual. In the end, the Freedmen's Bureau, like government treaties with the American Indians, served to discourage black Americans from making demands unacceptable at what may have been a difficult moment for the government, given that the domestic and international division caused by the Civil War was still salient196 and the ex-slaves had a limited supply of arms and were the majority population in important territorial areas (the so-called black belt stretching from the coast of South Carolina across to the Gulf of Mexico). It was, of course, impossible for the black minority to pressure the government to maintain its promises once the domestic situation was stabilized; thus, the Bureau was officially closed in 1872.

Whether the Freedmen's Bureau was the result of early demands by the black minority for the collective rights to economic reparation and local territorial autonomy, the pragmatic reaction to millions of freedmen flooding northern camps for assistance, or the result of the U.S. government toying with the idea of providing a degree of political autonomy to the black Americans,[97] is unclear.[98] If either was the case, neither became official U.S. policy.[99]

Transitional Period, Stage 2:
1868-1895 (The Reconstruction Period)

This period, which most black American scholars call Reconstruction, was more or less an unavoidable consequence of the situation resulting from a bitter Civil War and the effort to establish modern capitalism and national unity under northern control. While the idea of slavery had been officially discredited, no plan or proposal to meet the special needs (caused by their enslavement) of the black minority in order to obtain equal economic, social and political status with other Americans, was put forward. Although President Lincoln acknow-ledged the war against the south could not have been won without the military help of black Americans, W.E.B. DuBois, commenting on this admission, further noted:

The Afro-American, far from being the inert recipient of freedom at the hands of philanthropists, furnished 200,000 soldiers in the Civil War who took part in nearly 200 battles and skirmishes, and in addition, perhaps 300,000 others as effective laborers and helpers. In proportion to population, more black Americans than Anglo-Americans fought in the Civil War. These people, withdrawn from the support of the Confederacy, with the threat of the withdrawal of millions more, made the prolonged opposition of the slave holder almost impossible, unless they themselves freed and armed their enslaved Africans... They were restrained by realizing that such action removed the very cause for which the fighting began.

The reason for the U.S. failure to provide for the special equal status needs of the black minority can probably be seen in President Lincoln's less publicized attitude. While Lincoln may have supported the freeing of slaves and acknowledged the former slaves' aid in accomplishing that goal, his support for black American assimilation and civil rights was qualified, as evidenced by the following comments in a speech given August 21, 1858:

I will say, then, that I am not, nor ever have been in favor of bringing about, in any way, the social and political equality of the White and Black races; that I am not nor ever have been in favor of making voters or jurors of negroes, nor of qualifying them to hold office, nor to intermarry with white people; and I will say in addition to this that there is a physical difference between the white and black races which I believe will forever forbid the two races (from) living together on terms of social and political equality, and inasmuch as they cannot so live, while they do remain together there must be the position of superior and inferior, and I as much as any other man am in favor of having the superior position assigned to the white race.[200]

As the vague concept of black freedom was given concrete special measures neither legally nor constitutionally, and as a great part of Anglo-American sentiment was in fact ambivalent about the real meaning of the notion, actual policy remained pragmatic, balancing itself between rebel pressure, the interests of business and renewed economic stability, international environmental pressures,[201] and the willingness and capacity of black masses to politically define their needs and defend their recently acquired gains. Furthermore, the U.S. permitted the south to enact so-called "Black Codes" aimed at reestablishing for southern Anglo-Americans who accepted the idea of northern unity, their control and domination over the black minority. While few writers have ever suggested that this was part of the price paid by the north to end rebel resistance and obtain their cooperation, there is no logical reason to suggest that such an understanding was not reached. As a matter of fact, there is every reason to believe that the threat of a south politically dominated by the formerly enslaved Africans would have been a key card in the hand of victorious northerners seeking national unity and southern cooperation. The Black Codes drawn up by hastily organized state legislatures made up of ex-rebel Anglo-Americans who probably traded acceptance of the Union for Johnson's acquiescence to the codes, were passed during the Congressional recess. In the wake of the reaction of the African masses and likely moved by distrust of rebel loyalty to the union under the northern flag, the reconvened Congress made the concessions outlined in the preceding section and also, on March 23, 1867, passed the Reconstruction Act, which gave the vote to male black Americans, of whom nearly one million resided in the south.

The ramifications of this Act became most evident in the State of South Carolina, whose predominating black American population of 80,000 led to the election of a state legislature in 1868 in which black American delegates outnumbered Anglo-American delegates by

124 to 78. This legislature drew up a new constitution for the state, which was approved by a popular vote of 70,000 to 27,000 with 35,000 abstentions. This 1868 constitution heralded the beginnings of "The Reconstruction Period." The socialist orientation of the black minority can be seen in the 1868 Constitution, which abolished the Black Codes, protected civil rights, and gave the state its first system of free education.[202]

Having obtained not only the vote, but *the majority vote* in certain states, freedom for black Americans had been close. But faced with the spectre of black American predominance and hence political control of certain areas of the south, ex-rebel Anglo-Americans reavowed their allegiance to the Union, the northern flag, etc., and their resistance emerged in the form of paramilitary organizations whose purpose was to terrorize the black American population and thus in effect nullify the voting rights gained under the Reconstruction Act. In 1870, the Ku Klux Klan was formed and by 1875, the Red Shirts, Bush Wackers and the Night Riders, similar military/religious organizations designed to restore Anglo-American rule by force and violence, had emerged. Whippings, arson and murder in broad daylight became routine events. When Wade Hampton, a Democratic candidate, ran for the governorship of South Carolina in 1876, 2,000 Red Shirts "invaded" Hamburg, South Carolina to massacre a small black American militia company, thus forcing his election. They also looted and burned buildings owned by black Americans. When black American U.S. Congressional representatives in Washington demanded the help of federal troops, their efforts failed, even though some Congressmen supported them. Their return to the South to campaign for the re-election of liberal governors was rendered fruitless by the extra-legal tactics of the Anglo-American opposition.[203]

Finally, Reconstruction of the South under majority rule, "one man, one vote" was ended by President Rutherford B. Hayes, the l9th elected President of the United States, in 1877. He ordered all federal troops and military assistance to duly elected governments in the south to move out, leaving the black Americans there to protect themselves as best they could.[204] For millions of black Americans, the promise of freedom had come to an end. The Red Shirts, Jayhawkers and KKKs dominated the Democratic Party in the south. To return to our example of South Carolina, we find that by 1895, although the composition of the population had changed little since the earlier constitutional meeting of 1868, now only six of the 160 delegates were black Americans. By the end of 1895, a new constitution had been drawn up which repealed most of the black American rights established in 1868, and a new type of Black Codes was produced, the end product of which was segregation, which lasted officially until 1956. From 1895, the fate of black Americans' equal status and development went steadily downhill in all of the south until in 1903, the terror tactics of the KKK, the Red Shirts and other groups frightened black Americans from the ballot box, forced large numbers to leave the south, and ousted the last black Americans from state offices.

The essential meaning of this period for the USVCR was perhaps best summarized in President Theodore Roosevelt's December 3,1907 message. Roosevelt, like Lincoln, believed:

Nothing is more certainly written in the Book of Fate than that these people (black Americans) are to be free; and that it is no less certain that the two races (black Americans and Anglo-Americans), equally free, cannot live in the same government. Nature, habit, opinion have drawn indelible lines of distinction between them... (ie. if we must keep them in the same government, they cannot be equally free)

He further suggested that he:

had never seen a man, woman or child who was in favor of producing a perfect equality, social and political, between Negroes and White men. (Man, woman or child of course refers to Anglo-Americans.)205

Roosevelt (who was known for his Anglo-Saxon ethnocentralism) also often expressed the opinion that the Anglo-Saxon race was superior to all other races in Europe, Asia and Africa; thus, Anglo-Saxonization of the U.S. was viewed as practically a holy mission. However, it was toward the African peoples that he reserved his greatest disrespect. In 1895, following the breakdown of Reconstruction, he stated: "A perfectly stupid race can never rise to a very high plane. The Negro, for instance, has been kept down as much by lack of intellectual development as anything else." A Judge Advocate-General of Virginia carried Roosevelt's opinion to its logical conclusion, stating that "the whole problem of the south was whether the Negro or the White man should occupy the seat of power; whether the inferior should dominate the superior, and whether ignorance should rule intelligence."206 The recent observations of U.S. Supreme Court Justice Marshall corroborate our finding that such views became a part of U.S. policy towards national minorities:

> The status of the Negro as property was officially erased by his emancipation at the end of the Civil War. But the long awaited emancipation, while freeing the Negro from slavery, did not bring him citizenship or equality in any meaningful way. Slavery was replaced by a system of 'laws which imposed upon the colored race enormous disabilities and burdens and curtailed their rights in the pursuit of life, liberty, and property to such an extent that their freedom was of little value.' *Slaughter-House Cases*, 16 Wall. 36, 70 (1873). Despite the passage of the Thirteenth, Fourteenth and Fifteenth Amendments, the Negro was systematically denied the rights those amendments were supposed to secure. The combined actions and inactions of the State and Federal Governments maintained Negroes in a position of legal inferiority for another century after the Civil War.[207]

It was such notions and directions that determined the content of the USVCR until around 1960, which marked the legal end in America of apartheid. However, its essential conclusion, that the minority must be dominated and subordinated to majority politico-economic interest, may still remain, although the American government proved willing and able to employ practical and less oppressive means to achieve this end.

CHAPTER 3

BEGINNING OF POPULAR DISAFFECTION WITH THE DIRECTION OF THE ESTABLISHED "NEGRO" LEADERSHIP

1895-1960: THE APARTHEID PERIOD

Introduction

During this period, the early part of which is often referred to as the period of Jim Crow,[208] there was no basic change in the government's official attitude toward minority collective rights as they concerned its national minorities. No significant constitutional-legal changes were made in this period; the official minority concept represented in the institutions of segregation, which came into existence during the previous period following the breakdown of Reconstruction and the creation of new Black Codes, persisted legally until 1956 (*Brown v. Board of Education* case) and politically and socially until the late '60's. In 1956, the Supreme Court ruled indirectly that minority treatment under the institution of segregation was illegal; its actual ruling, however, ignoring and by-passing the notion of minorities altogether, was that segregation as an institution *affecting any American citizens* was unconstitutional.[209] Governmental implementation of this ruling began in the early 1960's under the Eisenhower, Kennedy and Johnson administrations.

This period is of specific interest, then, not because of any new development in the formulation of the USVCR, but because it is a period wherein black Americans made certain clearly defined and well-publicized demands regarding the type of collective future they wanted. A survey of these demands and the governmental response they were accorded will provide us with more information about which type of minority demands were ignored altogether by the majority, and which type received some support from liberal Anglo-Americans, thereby providing us with an idea of what the USVCR does and does not accept as legitimate possibilities. We shall survey only those central popular demands organized and supported by large segments of the black American minority, which have generally been recognized as significant by most scholars of the history of the black minority in the U.S..

The early part of this popular disaffection with the direction of the Negro leadership establishment was reflected in the mass support given to Marcus Garvey and the widespread intellectual recognition afforded W.E.B. DuBois. As these waves of disaffection changed to tides of discontent, they were galvanized by leaders such as Dr. Martin Luther King, Jr., The Honorable Elijah Muhammad, Malcolm X (El Hajj Malik El Shabazz), Stokley Carmichael and Rap Brown, to be taken up later by Jesse Jackson (the Rainbow Coalition) and Louis Farrakhan (The Nation of Islam), and numerous other smaller left, nationalist or civil rights progressive, third-world oriented groups (among them, we should note, the various Marxist groups and the New Republic of Africa). Although the U.S. government ignored the demands of most of these new challengers to the traditional negro leadership establishment, as we shall see in Chapter 4, the demands of Dr. Martin Luther King, Jr. to end apartheid (being more in line with the historical conditions of that moment) were able to galvanize enough popular domestic and international support to force the government to act to end apartheid in the southern states. However, before analyzing the historical conditions leading to King's victory and the meaning of that victory to the USVCR, let us mention a few of the earlier demands. This chapter will describe the earlier demands, and Chapter 4 will describe the historical conditions and circumstances leading to the popular victory against apartheid.

Minority Demands

The first of these popularly organized earlier demands to be advocated by significant segments of the black minority was, essentially, *a demand for population transfer* as a solution to the black American minority problem. This demand was quite similar to that earlier contemplated by Lincoln, certain elements of the federal government and the American Colonization Society.[210] However, this time it was galvanized by a member of the black minority itself, a man named Marcus Garvey. Although Garvey's rhetoric was often racist, the essence of his actual program for the black American minority was simply one of population transfer to Africa.

In 1920, Garvey founded the Universal Negro Improvement Association (UNIA) in New York, declared himself Provisional President of Africa, and convened his first so-called parliament, August lst, in the form of an international convention. Delegates to this convention endorsed the following goals set out by Garvey:

* to establish a universal confraternity among African peoples;
* to promote the spirit of pride and love;
* to administer to and assist the needy;
* to reclaim the fallen;
* to assist in civilizing the backward tribes of Africa;
* to assist in the development of independent African communities and nations;
* *to establish a central nation for Africans;*
* to establish commissaries or agencies in the principal countries and cities of the world for the representation of all Africans;
* to promote a conscientious spiritual worship among the native tribes of Africa;
* to establish universities, colleges, academies and schools for the education and culture of African peoples;
* to work for better conditions among Africans everywhere.211

For Garvey, the idea of establishing a central nation for all blacks meant the necessity of black Americans returning to Africa. This idea, like many of the other ideas in Garvey's program, was grotesquely out of tune with the real international politics of the period, during which the European world powers were in the process of extending their colonial empire in Africa. Nevertheless, the idea captured the imagination of many black Americans, and became the basis for the first popular mass political movement of the black minority in the U.S.. Using the slogans, "Africa for Africans" and "One God! One Aim! One Destiny!", he collected more money, an estimated ten million dollars in a two-year period, than any other black American political organization had ever done before. Garvey held conventions, organized factories, cooperatives, a small army, and even a merchant steamship line named "The Black Star Line."

Believing that Africa would have to be liberated from European domination in order for his dream to be realized, Garvey extended the UNIA by founding a series of paramilitary organizations: the Universal African Legion (of soldiers), the Universal African Motor Corps (of motorcycles and trucks), the Black Eagle Flying Corps, the Black Cross Nurses, and the Juveniles (similar to the Scout movements). He also founded the weekly newspaper *Negro World* (now the monthly magazine, *African World*), which he edited himself and filled with slogans such as "Africa for Africans" and "Renaissance of the African Race." These actions and statements having so aroused the hostility of European powers that Garvey realized the UNIA would never be legalized in any African colony which was European-controlled, he turned to Liberia as the sole independent West African country. Although he proposed to finance his project himself, negotiations with the Liberian government broke down; they correctly feared that he would attempt to take political control of the country and/or incite European forces in the surrounding states to attack.[212]

The sole known U.S. government response to the demands of the UNIA, the first popularly-voiced demands presented by the black minority in the U.S., was to arrest Garvey in 1923 on a charge of using the mails to defraud when raising money for his steamship line. Garvey was found guilty, and two years later was imprisoned in Atlanta to serve a five-year term. In 1927, however, President Coolidge pardoned him, and ordered his deportation as an undesirable alien. Garvey went to Jamaica and later to London, England where he died in 1940.

Garvey's knowledge of the international situation and of colonial and native conditions in Africa was extremely limited, and led him unintentionally to organize the financial resources and energies of millions of black Americans toward goals which were impractical and perhaps impossible for the time. Whether, given a cautious degree of recognition and cooperation, the plan might have become more realistic as a long-term project of the U.S. government, will remain unknown, for despite the interest of a significant segment of the black American minority in the basic concept of population transfer as a possible solution to their problem, the U.S. chose to completely ignore this possibility. Again, we suggest that the existing social separation and economic and political subordination of black American labour served the interest of American politico-economic development; this cheap labour reservoir would have been threatened by any population transfer scheme.[213] Again, therefore, what appears to have been a significant effort at minority self-expression was thwarted by the unyielding wall of majority interest.[214]

However, when a black American leader such as Booker T. Washington (1858-1915) emerged with policies which posed no threat to majority interest, he gained nation-wide recognition among Anglo-Americans, even though there was no evidence that he represented popular aspirations of any sizable following in the black American minority.[215] Washington's advocacy of the concepts of social separation and political and economic subordination was no doubt due to his belief that bending to the will of a powerful majority might eventually arouse such sympathy and sense of injustice in the majority that, in the long run, the best interests of the black minority would be served. However, Washington's reasons aside, the sentiments he expressed were acceptable to Anglo-Americans, and thenceforth were given symbolic official recognition in Washington's posthumous election to the American Hall of Fame in 1945 for his contributions to the education of 'young' people.

The ideas of Washington were most directly opposed by another black American leader of the period, Dr. W.E.B. DuBois (1868-1964). Born in Great Barrington, Massachusetts, into a comfortable middle-class family, he earned his B.A. and M.A. at Fisk, his Ph.D. at Harvard, and did post-doctoral research at the University of Berlin. While Garvey represented the popular masses, DuBois was an intellectual, and excelled in classroom teaching and in writing. While being mainly active against the philosophy of Washington, he was also opposed to Garvey's African zionism. DuBois fathered the idea of Pan-Africanism, which was to serve as a political philosophy and guide to action for Africans in Africa who were laying the foundations of national liberation. While Garvey resented European exploitation of Africa and campaigned in his "Back to Africa" movement to remove European domination from Africa, he believed firmly in capitalism. On the other hand, DuBois opposed transplanting black Americans to Africa, and was a staunch advocate of complete self-government for Africans in Africa organized on the basis of socialism and a co-operative economy. Most importantly, DuBois attacked Booker T. Washington's creed on the general basis that until the dominant group sees its best material interest as being bound up with the best interest of the black American minority, the latter's situation was hopeless.[216]

In his efforts to side with the interests of the masses of oppressed blacks, DuBois became a rallying figure for the so-called black middle-class militants of the period. In 1905, he and William Monroe Trotter, a well-known black American journalist, held a conference of the so-called black minority intelligentsia, later dubbed "the Talented Tenth," in Niagara Falls, Canada. This conference assembled a group of radical, middle-class black Americans for the first time, and provided them with a common platform based on Dr. DuBois' eight point program:

* Freedom of speech and criticism
* An unfettered and unsubsidized press
* Manhood suffrage
* The abolition of all American caste distinctions based simply on race and color

* The recognition of the principles of human brotherhood as a practical creed
* The recognition of the highest and best known training as the monopoly of no class or race
* A belief in the dignity of labor
* United effort to realize these ideals under wise and courageous leadership.

Adopting this program, conferees evolved into the "Niagara Movement," a new black minority organization which opposed U.S. apartheid. The liberals of abolitionist days and many Jewish Americans threw in their lot with the Niagarans to form the National Association for the Advancement of Colored People (NAACP). In 1915, DuBois founded the NAACP magazine, *The Crisis,* which he edited himself until 1932. This magazine became the chief medium through which the NAACP's campaign for the advancement of the black minority was promoted. The NAACP, by definition never a popularly-based black minority movement, found increasing acceptance among American liberals who, by cooperating with its objectives and in turn receiving compromises turning the organization against the evolving progressive and socialist ideas of its founder, Dr. DuBois, made it the accepted vehicle through which a continuing struggle against apartheid and for assimilation would be fought.[217] The NAACP opposed all other popularly-based movements in the black community that did not share its assimilationist ideals. This organization, the most acceptable to Anglo-American liberals, did not suffer from the potential of limiting the supply of cheap black minority labour to the American business community.[218] However, it did create some of the moral and legal conditions which permitted Dr. Martin Luther King, Jr. to mobilize the traditional negro leadership establishment in favor of non-violent action.

Around the 1930's, a new form of black resistance to the traditional "negro" leadership establishment emerged, this time in the form of religion.[219] Although this was not the first time religion's resistance to traditional leadership has occurred on the U.S. national scene, [220] (there were continuous Islamic revolts against slavery, as documented in the now popular book, "Roots") it was the first time such a movement was to gain, by the early '60's, significant popular support among black Americans. The existence of the movement was credited to a man called W.D. Fard. Said to have been born in Mecca in 1877, the son of a wealthy member of the Qureysh tribe of which the Prophet Muhammad (sallahu alaihi wassallam) himself had been a member, Fard is reputed to have been educated in England, and to have been trained for a diplomatic career in the Kingdom of Hejaz in the Arabian peninsula. These facts, however, have never been confirmed. When Fard reached the United States in 1930, presumably to continue his studies, he proclaimed that his mission was to secure freedom, justice and equality for his 'uncle' (the black minority) living in the wilderness of North America and under the control of Anglo-Americans. The advent of an Islamic movement was new to the American scene. It was also difficult to understand. First, it was assumed by Americans that the Islamic religion of many of the enslaved Africans had been destroyed during the slave period. While this assumption was essentially true, there were significant exceptions relating to the immigration or importation, for various reasons, of enslaved Africans after the official end of slavery. Second, Americans had no acquaintance with a religion that does not separate its political, economic and social spheres from religious affairs. Therefore, most of the early analysis tended not to regard the American Islamic movement as essentially a religious movement because of its attention to the problems of black American oppression. The deep and devout adherence of the early Islamic converts was treated more as a radical political commitment than a religious devotion. This was probably because black Christian scholars did not understand or believe the degree of their disbelief in the King James version of the Bible and absolute belief in the Quran. Also, American intellectuals being removed or unaware of events taking place in the Islamic world, had little basis for understanding what was happening in relation to Islam among U.S. blacks. While many U.S. blacks (and additionally Franz Fanon and Marcus Garvey) had been exposed to the new direction of the Islamic reawakening toward an identification with and defence of the cause of the world's oppressed,[22] American intellectuals, both black and white, were barely aware that Islam existed.

This new movement represented perhaps the more radical resistance against the traditional negro leadership establishment and the black Anglo-American values and culture promoted by that leadership. Most important, it represented the first popular effort by blacks in the U.S. to revolt against the unorthodox protestant slave-culture-influenced interpretation of the King James version of the Bible, and thus against the slave-based values of their historical orientation .

The Islamic movement in the U.S. became popular after Fard disappeared and Elijah Muhammad (1897-1975) popularized the movement among black Americans. Elijah Muhammad was born on a tenant farm in Sandersville, Georgia.222 As Dr. Essien Udom, a Nigerian lecturer who taught at Harvard and Brown universities, wrote: "Little is known about his early life but that he worked as a field boy, a railroad laborer, and for a sawmill and brick manufacturer before 1919, when he migrated to Detroit with his wife and two children." In Detroit, he met Fard, and the movement began in earnest.

By 1945, Elijah Muhammad's movement was the largest Muslim community in the United States and he had begun reaching for the leadership of the total black minority in the U.S.. While many of his slogans fell victim to the prevalent American racist orientation,223 his general philosophy was based on the belief that since Anglo-Americans were historically the political, economic and cultural adversaries of the black Americans, their opposition to Muslim policies was to be expected. However, he believed that this acceptance of Anglo-American hostility made it possible for Muslim leaders to express the interests of the black minority and become the most advanced and resolute section within the black minority, and therefore destined to push all other sections ahead. Black Americans would follow, he believed, because the Muslims had clearer understanding of where they wanted to go, and of the conditions necessary to achieve ultimate results. His movement also felt that the ultimate aims of Muslim leaders were virtually identical to those of all black Americans:

* the unity of black Americans (which for the Muslims probably meant encouraging most black Americans to accept Islam)
* the destruction of Anglo-American cultural and economic domination over the black American communities (expressed as a need for separation into autonomous states; however, Muslim political development had not yet moved to the point of seeing the notion of domination as resulting from the necessities of a capitalist politico-economic system)
* the acquisition of representative political power in the government of the United States (representative political power meaning, to this group, the control of a few states in the south.)

During this period 1900-1956, the official U.S. reaction was to ignore these demands for a separate black American state, a separate cultural and political identity, and eventual independence from the U.S., and to apply the law equally to Muslims as they would to any American. When Elijah Muhammad set up a parochial school for Muslims and placed his own child in it, he was charged with contributing to the delinquency of a minor. In 1942, Elijah was arrested in Washington, D.C., this time for sedition and inciting Muslims to resist the draft.224 The charge of sedition was dropped, but he was sentenced to five years in prison for the other charge. Returning from prison after this period of apartheid, he continued the development of his Islamic movement until he died in 1975. His son, Warid Muhammad, succeeded him in continuing this Islamic development. In 1981, the movement was split between the leadership of Warid Muhammad and that of his ex-Chief Minister, Louis Farrakhan. Both divisions of his movement today are internationally oriented and have succeeded to some degree in placing the question of the black American identity as a concern of other Islamic and non-Islamic nations.225 The Honorable Elijah Muhammad himself is no longer seen by American Muslims as a prophet but more as a teacher whose mission was to demonstrate to his people that the Bible was not necessarily correct and was used by the Anglo-Americans to oppress them. His adherence to the actual teachings of Islam is universally questioned.

Conclusion

The central point brought to light in this chapter is that the U.S. was confronted with various types of minority demands during this period, demands which varied significantly and had differing degrees of support within the black minority. A degree of official recognition was extended only to those representing the philosophy of B.T. Washington, who was permitted to establish the Tuskegee Institute (a school for blacks), which became an example for the black minority's segregated education system. Also a certain amount of unofficial and official juridical recognition was given to the program of the NAACP in the north. As ideas and demands from the other popular groups were ignored, it is a strong probability that the U.S. government felt that the national minority had no other rights than those which also served the interest of the majority, as defined by members of the majority. Professor Derrick A. Bell, Jr., in his article "Racial Remediation," states the same idea this way:

But even a rather cursory look at American legal history suggests that in the past, the most significant political advances for blacks resulted from policies which were extended and had the effect of serving the interests and convenience of whites rather than remedying racial injustices against blacks. This conclusion is justified even though the actions had a liberating effect.

Also U.S. Supreme Court Justice Powell clearly affirms the continuing influence of this U.S. policy orientation when he announced the judgment of the court in the Bakke Case, stating:

The concepts of 'majority' and 'minority' necessarily reflect temporary arrangements and political judgments. As observed above, the white 'majority' itself is composed of various minority groups, most of which can lay claim to a history of prior discrimination at the hands of the state and private individuals. Not all of these groups can receive preferential treatment and corresponding judicial tolerance of distinctions drawn in terms of race and nationality, for then the only 'majority' left would be a new minority of White Anglo-Saxon Protestants. There is no principled basis for deciding which groups would merit 'heightened judicial solicitude' and which would not.

The subjective and psychologically stressful effects of the USVCR, as reflected in the above citation (which ignored the existence of national minorities' unique needs and demands *vis-à-vis* the majority) were perhaps best poetically expressed in 1952 by the well-known novelist, Ralph Ellison in his novel, *The Invisible Man*. He wrote:

I am invisible, understand, simply because people refuse to see me, like the bodiless heads you see sometimes in circus side shows. It is as though I have been surrounded by mirrors of hard, distorted glass. When they (AngloAmericans) approach me, they see only my surroundings, themselves, or fragments of their imagination. Indeed, everything and anything but me.

CHAPTER 4

THE ERA OF MARTIN LUTHER KING, JR.

1960~1975: THE CONTEMPORARY PERIOD

This chapter is not written to describe Martin Luther King, Jr.'s movement but to present the historical systemic conditions that made possible his legal victory against the U.S. institution of segregation, and to analyze the meaning of that victory in regard to the general USVCR. This period was ushered in by the *Brown v. Board of Education* Court Decision which led to the official dismantlement of legal apartheid in the U.S.. During this period 1960-1975, the evolution of the USVCR, particularly concerning the black American minority, must be viewed in the light of three important factors: the historical changes occurring in the international situation which influenced the domestic American scene, the growing minority protest through the non-violent civil rights campaigns, and the Islamic rnovements, and through violent riots, and the adjustability of the USVCR to the changed domestic and international environments

Changes in the International Environment
in Relation to the American Domestic Situation

Between the time that U.S. apartheid was being organized in the early 1900's and the visible impact of the *Brown v. Board of Education* decision around 1964, virtually a slow revolution had taken place in the international system. The U.S.S.R. had achieved nuclear parity with the U.S., the Third World nations (once the formal colonies of Europe) had emerged as an independent world voice; the Monroe Doctrine had been successfully challenged by Cuba and the U.S.S.R.; and the U.S. military, moral and economic superiority had been called into question by Vietnam on the one hand, and on the other, by the increasing desire of Europe to emerge from under U.S. economic domination and play its own role on the new world stage.

This change in power relations was reflected in the United Nations and in the new U.N. emphasis on collective rights. In December 1960, the General Assembly adopted Resolution 395 (V) which expressed the opinion that "a policy of 'racial segregation' (apartheid)

is necessarily based on doctrines of racial discrimination."226 Resolution 721 (VIII) of December 8, 1953 and Resolution 320 (IX) of December 14, 1954 expressed the strong conviction that these policies (policies of racial segregation and apartheid) endangered friendly relations among states (Section VIII) and constituted a grave threat to the peaceful relations between ethnic groups in the world. The success of these resolutions by the General Assembly, being pushed by the Third World and socialist bloc, led to the passing of Resolution 1761 (XVII) on November 6, 1962, which called on all members of the United Nations to take action against states practicing racial apartheid. The resolutions 721 (VIII) and 320 (IX) occurred two and three years before the U.S. officially ended formal apartheid. and more than five years before the policy was actually implemented.227

By the end of 1972, again with the initiative coming from the Third World nations in conjunction with the socialist bloc countries, the following major declarations relating to collective human rights were adopted by the General Assembly:

* Declaration on the granting of independence to colonial countries and peoples; proposals for a Declaration on the Rights of Peoples and Nations to Self-Determination were made to the General Assembly; the U.S.S.R. presented the first concrete proposal in1955 ;228
* Declaration on the Elimination of All Forms of Racial Discrimination (1963).

The following major covenants, conventions and protocols were in force by the end of this period under investigation (1960-1975):

* the Convention on the Prevention and Punishment of the Crime of Genocide (adopted 1945) came into force on January 12, 1951;
* the supplementary convention on the abolition of slavery, the slave trade, and institutions and practices similar to slavery was adopted in 1956, coincidentally the same year as the historic *Brown* decision;
* the International Convention on the Elimination of All Forms of Racial Discrimination entered into force on January 4, 1969;
* the Optional Protocol to the International Covenant on Civil and Political Rights was adopted by the General Assembly in 1966; it provided individuals and groups with the right to present complaints before the Human Rights Committees of the United Nations.

Although the Covenant came into force after the period being discussed (1977), the Optional Protocol is presently not in force.

These manifestations of world opinion were difficult for the U.S. to ignore. Since the end of World War 11, she had been locked in a struggle with communist powers for the loyalty of the newly-emergent ex-colonial Third World nations. Since most of the former colonies were non-white and therefore highly sensitive to any sign of U.S. racism, this consideration obliged American foreign policy elites to reckon with the international costs of a segregated domestic order. The federal court presiding over the *Brown v. Board of Education* case was made fully aware of the relation between America's domestic policies and her foreign policy interests in the federal government's *Amicus Curiae* brief, which read:

It is in the context of the present world struggle between freedom and tyranny that the problem of racial discrimination must be viewed... (for) discrimination against minority groups in the United States has an adverse effect upon our relations with other countries. Racial discrimination furnishes grist for the communist propaganda mills, and it raises doubts even among friendly nations as to the intensity of our devotion to the democratic faith.229

The near coincidence of U.N. resolutions against apartheid in 1953 and 1954, and the 1956 *Brown v. Board of Education* ruling which led to the official ending of American apartheid, and of the 1966 Optional Protocol and the U.S. Civil Rights Act of 1968, may indicate that the pressure of U.S. foreign policy interests influenced her domestic civil rights policy decisions. Domestic and foreign human rights policy could no longer be separated as in the past.

Domestic policy, however, was subjected to more pressures than simply that of the American foreign policy goal of maintaining alliances and winning friends abroad. When the black American soldier returned home from World War II, Korea and Vietnam, his horizons expanded by his experience of the absence of many of those social barriers in foreign nations that he would have encountered at home, like other black Americans who had begun to travel and take interest in international events, he became increasingly aware of the contradictions between the ideal and the actual in American life, between the negro leadership's illusions and the U.S. establishment's real direction in a society where he could not attend the school of his choice, drink from certain fountains, nor eat at Anglo-American restaurants. Again, as following the Civil War, the presence and potential threat of black militants, particularly ex-soldiers with military experience gained through helping the federal government in war, and with the heightened awareness and expectations arising therefrom, began to merge with the general discontent of the masses around 1960 to exert its obvious influence. But now, due to industrialization, the scene had changed. Industrialization, having unsettled much of the old negro rural caste system of the south by encouraging an increased migration of rural black Americans to the urban centers, had uprooted black Americans and exposed them to new patterns of living. Individuals in urban areas, less encumbered by older ways of relating with the majority (the values of African slave-generated culture) and in closer proximity, were now more open to socio-political mobilization. The anticipation of black unrest in combination with the changed international environment led first to a practical effort of the U.S. to make the policy of segregation acceptable (e.g. separate and equal), and when this did not work, to finally abandon segregation in favor of other policies.

However, when President Truman first attempted legislation which would prohibit the poll tax,[230] put an end to segregation in transportation, and set up a Fair Employment Practices Commission, his proposals died in Congress, mostly at the hands of a Senate which had very strong southern representation, which was blind to the international changes. The President's activism was not appreciated by southern politicians. As far as they were concerned, Truman had gone much too far in the legislative programs. When he decided to stand for election in 1948, many southern democrats walked out of that year's nominating convention. They proceeded to form the Dixiecrat party, and nominated Strom Thurmond of South Carolina as their presidential candidate. This act by many Anglo-American politicians from the south, severing their loyalty from the national party, demonstrated only too well the resistance to changes in the USVCR as it then was, ie. apartheid .

The Eisenhower administration continued practical political efforts along the lines laid down by Truman. In 1957 and 1960, it pushed through acts empowering the attorney-general to seek court injunctions whenever voting rights were infringed upon, founded a Commission on Civil Rights, and created a Civil Rights Division in the Justice Department. The major provision of the 1960 bill enabled judges to aid black Americans (or any U.S. citizens) in registering and voting. Finally, during President Eisenhower's tenure of office, federal troops were sent south to enforce public desegregation for the first time since the Civil War.[231]

Minority Protest

An important consideration for evaluating the pragmatism and changes in the USVCR (1960-1975) is to understand the strength of the impetus for change provided by the black national minority itself. As the judicial process was not fast enough to keep pace with black American demands, the new tactic of massive resistance to laws deemed unjust was enunciated by the Reverend Martin Luther King, Jr. and those who followed him. This new tendency to rely upon mass pressures for immediate alterations in the status quo, rather than on the court, led to an increasing mobilization of southern Anglo-Americans as well as black Americans in defense of their perceived interests and to a general systemic political crisis for the government.[232]

King and other anti-apartheid black leaders sought to appeal to the good will of the great majority of people in the U.S. and in the world in their effort to strike down Jim Crow statutes, by appealing to a higher law than the laws of the Anglo-American majority: that of the equality of man before God. God's law was deemed to be binding on both ethnies. Strong elements of the Anglo-American majority argued, however, that it is always evil to break existing laws, and that any change must come through proper legal or legislative channels. As the opposing sides saw reality, and hence legitimacy, through such differing lenses, peaceful compromise in the U.S. ethnic confrontations became exceedingly difficult.

Discord between the minority and majority ethnic groups accelerated rapidly in the years immediately preceding the passage of the Civil Rights Act of 1964. The first sit-in occurred in Greensboro, North Carolina in February 1960,[233] when college students at North Carolina Agricultural and Technical College protested against racial discrimination at the local dime store counter. The technique quickly spread to other cities and towns, and the sit-in became a major weapon in the struggle against apartheid. The following year, another technique was applied: buses carrying "Freedom Riders" drove through the south to test segregation in bus terminals. The rides were marred by much racial tension and some violence along the route.[234] Anti-apartheid advocates increased their actions in defiance of U.S. traditions and laws when many of their opponents refused to yield and instead turned to violence against the Afro-American protesters. Protests often ended in bloodshed and mass arrests.

As the conflict began to be perceived as one of zero-sum, not mutual adjustment of interest, Islamic religious, nationalist and radical revolutionary elements of the black minority, the Black Panthers, the New Republic of Africa, the Blood Brothers, the Mau Mau, the OAAU, the Hannafi's, etc.235 began to enter the mainstream of the political arena. Beginning in early spring and extending into the summer of 1963, a plethora of sit-ins, boycotts, demonstrations and violent ethnic conflicts, including well-publicized beatings and even murders took place. Medgar Evers, head of the Mississippi branch of the NAACP was shot in Jackson, Mississippi, and a black American high school in Mississippi was bombed. In response, the early riots of 1963-64 began, occurring through a wide span of American cities, both northern and southern.236 During these riots, the police and national guards used guns, tear gas, dogs, etc. while the black minority used rocks, Molotov cocktails, etc.. Concomitant with the riots, some 800 cities and towns were struck by demonstrations. The year was climaxed by the massive August "March on Washington" by some 200,000 American citizens to pressure Congress into enacting new civil rights legislation that would end official and unofficial apartheid. In 1964, the Civil Rights Act proposed by Kennedy was passed under Johnson.

However, the Civil Rights Act of 1964 was addressed essentially to middle-class needs. There was no demand to alter the economic status quo, but rather for the civil rights legally guaranteed to any American to be extended to individual members of America's national minorities. The right to service in restaurants and motels, etc. was primarily of benefit to those relatively well-off minority assimilationists seeking Anglo-American values and advantages. For the masses of blacks in the ghettos of American cities, the middle-class victory did little to alleviate the basic circumstances affecting their lives.237

Sparked by the assassination of Martin Luther King, Jr. in 1965 and the teachings of Malcolm X, etc., the riots continued, increasing in both intensity and scope.238 The majority ethnicity added units of the U.S. army and spotter planes; the black American minority added snipers to its arsenal of rocks and Molotov cocktails. As a reading of the report by the National Advisory Commission on Civil Disorders set up by President Johnson shows, the spontaneous uprisings which occurred were similar in intensity and ethnic hatred to the slave revolts just before the Civil War.238

The potential of prolonged rioting in major American cities in relation to the new international environment, provoked a profound systemic crisis and impelled government reaction. This reaction came in 1968, in the form of yet another Civil Rights Act. Once again, the intensity of minority protest was able to arouse the government to take action; whether that action, however, was a well-thought-out solution to the minority problem, or simply a pragmatic response intended merely to stave off further minority protest, will be elaborated in the following section. It suffices here to say that controlling the riots and preventing a prolonged continuous period of disorder was no doubt of uppermost importance to the U.S. in order to maintain its international image and influence in the way that image may affect influence, and influence affect international power. A continuous prolonged period of majority-minority conflict might also have provided the diplomatic leverage needed by political enemies of the U.S. to muster a drive for a United Nations verbal or moral intervention in the domestic U.S. minority problem.[240] With the black minority divided as it was between Muslims, nationalists,[241] civil rights reformers,[242] and sincere revolutionaries,[243] those pushing for U.N. intervention would have enlisted the support of a significant element within the black American minority. It is unthinkable that the U.S. government would have done anything that might permit this possibility to occur.

The Pragmatic Adjustment of the USVCR to the New Domestic and International Environments

Though the pressures elaborated above compelled governmental reaction, counter pressures were at work to try to prevent any substantial changes in the USVCR that might threaten majority interests as conceived by certain subgroups of the majority, ie. the Anglo-American-dominated south. Ironically, the ultimate passage of the strong civil rights bill in 1964 to systematically reinterpret and process black American demands, was aided legislatively by Lyndon B. Johnson's elevation to the presidency and by the strong national division caused by Kennedy's assassination. As a southerner and so-called moderate on the issue of apartheid, not completely trusted by any spokesmen within the black minority or within the liberal constituency of the Democratic party, he chose to come forth immediately against the policy of segregation.[244]

The provisions of the bill Johnson presented brought about a momentous debate. The bill facilitated voting by the black American minority by making a sixth-grade education sufficient for literary purposes; it enabled the attorney-general to file suits to force school integration; and it denied federal funds to states, schools or other organizations which continued to practice apartheid. Through an Equal Employment Opportunity section, it outlawed discrimination in much of the business and labor world. It sanctioned access, regardless of race, to such owner-operated facilities as lunchrooms, restaurants, theaters, hotels, stadiums and large rooming houses, and to enforce this access to public accommodations, it empowered the attorney general to bring suit when such rights were violated.

While the Bill's contents struck harshly at the basic values of many Americans, such as the rectitude of subordinating and segregating black Americans, the sanctity of the concept of private property and the idealized right of owners to exercise practically unlimited control over their property,[245] neither business nor labor joined the struggle to resist its passage.[246] Leading Republicans and Democrats alike were agreed on the necessity of federal action in the civil rights field to keep violence in a community now influenced on one hand by King and on the other by Elijah Muhammad, to a minimum. The main thrust of opposition to the bill came from the Anglo-American south,[248] which feared that the black population in that area was sufficiently large to be able to claim through voting a political power similar to that they had attained following the Reconstruction acts of the late 1860's. The final outcome of this conflict of interest within the majority, where southern irrational, racist resistance battled against the U.S.' real foreign and domestic policy need to end apartheid, was the passage of the 1964 Civil Rights Act, a revindication of the national majority interest.

The Supreme Court had already entered the struggle on the side of the Executive Division of government, ie. the federal side, where national interest overrode state interest. In 1954, the Court had ruled in *Brown v. Board of Education* that segregation of public schools was unconstitutional. This decision, upsetting the practice long established in the south and reversing an 1896 ruling *(Plessy v. Ferguson)*, thrust the judiciary into a policy realm where Congress and the Senate (both with strong southern representation) had been unwilling or unable to move. The Court prohibited segregation in transportation facilities involved in interstate commerce; it also doomed restrictive covenants which had previously given legal standing to private agreements preventing the sale of property to black Americans. Following the series of sit-ins and demonstrations which began in 1960, the Court on various grounds decided in favor of those who had been denied access to restaurants and other places of public accommodation.

The thrust of these actions by both the Congress and the Judiciary, however, was simply to extend the coverage of existing civil rights for American citizens to include coverage for individuals of the American national minorities. As such, it served rather as window dressing to brighten America's tarnished image as a land of freedom and equality, than as a viable approach for granting equal status rights to minorities or solving minority problems. As Derrick Bell observed:

... judicial relief is more likely to be forthcoming if the complaint of activities are also damaging and embarrassing to the country 's stated ideals... The relief actually granted by the Civil Rights Acts of 1964-68 tends primarily to improve the country's democratic image and only secondarily or collaterally to repay the harm which initially prompted the litigation, and subsequent non-racial decisions relying on the initial civil rights precedent often bring greater substantive benefit to the community at large than was obtained by black Americans.249

The unwillingness of the federal government to embark upon any sort of conceptual reorientation that might facilitate a solution to minority economic, political and social inequality was reflected in the very approach of a report by the National Advisory Commission on Civil Disorders set up by President Lyndon B. Johnson on July 29, 1967. While this was the second governmental agency established to deal exclusively with the problem of America's chief national minority,250 the Commission refused to officially recognize the existence of this minority in outlining its task. Its official task was stated as being to seek the reasons of civil disorder, as if it were occurring among the general U.S. population. The section of the report called the Commission Task read:

Much of the report is directed to the condition of those Americans who are also negroes, and to the social and economic environment in which they live. But this nation is confronted with the issue of justice for all its people, white as well as black, rural as well as urban. In particular, we are concerned for those who have continued to keep faith with society in the preservation of public order, the people of Spanish surname, the American Indians, and other minority groups to whom this country owes respect. By focusing on the negro, we do not mean to imply any priority of need... When we speak of the negro, we do not speak of 'them', we speak of 'us'.

This attempt to play down or ignore the ethnic revolt for equal status aspect of the conflict (and thus ignore the central problem) was in line with Johnson's special appeal to the members of the Commission to be non-political.251 Thus, though the report in fact deals almost exclusively with the history and social conditions of the black minority in the U.S., documenting the most serious violent conflicts between the U.S. majority and the national minority occurring from 1963-1970, it only indirectly tells us that the general cause of these hundreds of riots was the historical pattern of relational inequality existing between the black and Anglo-American.[252] This refusal to recognize or accept the reality of U.S. history -- that only a scant eleven years ago, the American constitutional and legal system had officially permitted a separate and unequal policy of segregation towards its chief national minority -- is doubly punitive to the black American minority: first by mystifying its present situation through denying historical causality, and consequently secondly, by shifting the responsibility for the situation on 'the moving apart' or on those who sought to struggle for equal status. The denial of the special historical circumstances which pertain to the problems of the black American minority serves to prevent this minority from being distinguished in any (positive) way from the general population in the future, and to refute in advance any demands for affirmative action, quotas, etc. or special measures or protective rights *vis-à-vis* the majority that it might require to obtain equal economic, social and political status.

While the U.S. non-discrimination and integration theory evidenced by the civil rights acts of 1964 and 1968 holds that once U.S. society reaches a state of complete non-discrimination and integration, the black minority and all other minority problems will be solved, there was little evidence by the end of this period 1960-1975 that such was indeed the case.[253] As a matter of fact, the most recent surveys of 1985 state that the inequalities between the masses of black Americans and Anglo-Americans have dramatically increased. Though national interest ceased to focus attention upon the black minority once the riots stopped and the 1968 civil rights act was apparently accepted as meeting minority demands and needs, the position of the black minority *vis-à-vis* the majority, far from improving, actually worsened.[254] The re-stabilization of the political system subsequent to the riots appears to represent a return to the constants in U.S. minority-majority relations.[255] The changes which occurred in the USVCR during the period 1960-1975 were not necessarily the result of a change in the basic philosophy of the U.S. government,[256] but rather the result of the U.S. capacity to act pragmatically when confronted with a serious political crisis. On June 27, 1978, U.S. Supreme Court Justice Marshall, in dissenting from the 4/5 slip decision of the U.S. Supreme Court in the *University of California v. Allan Bakke* case stated:

I fear that we have come full circle. After the Civil War our government started several 'affirmative action' programs. This Court in the Civil Rights

Cases and *Plessy v. Ferguson* destroyed the movement toward complete equality. For almost a century no action was taken, and this nonaction was with the tacit approval of the courts. Then we had *Brown v. Board of Education* and the Civil Rights Acts of Congress, followed by numerous affirmative action programs. Now, we have this Court again stepping in, this time to stop affirmative action programs of the type used by the University of California.

The position of the Negro today in America is the tragic but inevitable consequence of centuries of unequal treatment. Meaningful equality remains a distant dream for the Negro.

A Negro child today has a life expectancy which is shorter by more than five years than that of a white child. The Negro child's mother is over three times more likely to die of complications in childbirth, and the infant mortality rate for Negroes is nearly twice that for whites. The median income of the Negro family is only 609~ that of the median of a white family... For Negro adults, the unemployment rate is twice that of whites, and the unemployment rate for Negro teenagers is nearly three times that of white teenagers. A Negro male who completes four years of college can expect a median annual income of merely $110 more than a white male who has only a high school diploma. Although Negroes represent 11.596 of the population, they are only 1.2% of the lawyers and judges, 2% of the physicians, 2.3% of the dentists, 1.1% of the engineers, and 2.6% of the college and university professors.257

CONCLUSION

Historical Summary, ILVCR

The question of minorities in Islamic civilization, which was concerned primarily with religious minorities[259], predates that of minority concerns within western civilization by over six centuries. In western civilization, the question of minorities arose in sixteenth century Europe, along with the contemporary State system. Thus as territorial political sovereignty gradually replaced religious, ethnic and family ties as the basis of political organization, an inevitable result was the creation of ethnic majorities and minorities.[260] Since frontiers often divided the members of particular groups, the treatment of minorities in one State was sometimes given as the reason for intervention by its neighbors.[261] This of course created early international concern over the protection of minorities in international relations and law. These concerns increased with the consolidation of the multinational state system in Europe.

Treaty provisions dealing with the protection of European minorities, especially religious minorities, began to appear in European and European-Turkish relations by the mid-seventeenth century. A complex network of such treaties governed the Balkan region from the mid-nineteenth century until the First World War. Following the World War, the League of Nations supervised a new network of treaties for the protection of the minorities divided by the frontiers of newly-independent Eastern and Central European states.[262] These treaties provided, *inter alia,* for non-discrimination, and cultural and educational autonomy.[263]

The first international efforts to establish general norms for the protection of all minorities, rather than minorities in particular countries, were not to arise until the drafting of the International Covenants of Human Rights in the 1950s. This is true although, as earlier mentioned, a general conception of protected groups *(dhimma)* had long existed in Islamic law, and enabled Muslim states to govern extremely cosmopolitan, religiously diverse territories.[264]

Given the domestic situation of the emerging world power, the U.S.A., minorities were not mentioned in the peace treaties concluding the Second World War, with two exceptions[265], nor at all in the Charter of the United Nations or the Universal Declaration of

Human Rights. The Secretariat, in 1947, took the view that the League's minorities system as a whole had "ceased to exist", in favor of a new universal and individualistic conception of human rights,266 one which conformed to the needs of the U.S. minorities policies of forced cultural assimilation in relation to European minorities, and one which tended to ignore the human rights of non-European minorities.

However, with the pressure of the socialist states, the Economic and Social Council authorized the newly-created Commission on Human Rights to make recommendations regarding the "protection of minorities", and then approved the establishment, in 1947, of the Sub-Commission, with minority rights and non-discrimination as its mandate.267 In 1948 the General Assembly expressed concern over the "fate of minorities" in a resolution adopted the same day as the Universal Declaration of Human Rights, and invited the Commission to make a "thorough study of the problem of minorities, in order that the United Nations may be able to take effective measures for the{ir} protection."268 The following year, the Commission clarified the mandate of the Sub-Commission and reaffirmed its authority to undertake studies in this field.269

In 1950, the Sub-Commission completed its draft of what was to become article 27 of the International Covenant on Civil and Political Rights: *Persons belonging to ethnic, religious or linguistic minorities shall not be denied the right, in community with the other members of their group, to enjoy their own culture, to profess and practise their own religion, or to use their own language.* 270 The Commission approved this text after inserting the phrase, "in those States in which ethnic, religious or linguistic minorities exist." The addition was explained as necessary to distinguish newly-immigrated groups and indigenous people.271 We should note that the U.S. government claims that no minorities exist in the U.S. since everyone was an immigrant in the process of assimilation.

A number of technical studies of the legal status and classification of minorities were undertaken between 1948 and 1955 by the Sub-Commission.272 In 1968, the Sub-Commission, noting "the difficulty of establishing a general definition of minorities," proposed a new study of "the concept of minorities".273 This task was entrusted to Francesco Capotorti in 1971, and his report, which was discussed earlier in more detail, helped to stimulate interest in drafting a declaration of principles "on the rights of persons belonging to national, ethnic, religious and linguistic minorities." An open-ended working group of the Commission was established for this purpose in

1978.274 It appears that the U.S. intends to have this declaration interpreted or written so as to exclude equal consideration of non-European minorities, and to focus rather on Jewish and other minorities in Eastern Europe.

Work on the draft declaration has continued through the forty-fifth session of the Commission.275 The preamble and four substantive articles have been adopted provisionally thus far; three proposed articles remain to be considered. The adopted articles deal with non-discrimination of minorities, freedom from attacks upon their existence or their rights, promotion of their cultures and identity, and freedom of expression and communication, domestically and internationally.

While the U.S.' efforts may suggest that a general definition of "minorities" has not yet been adopted, a listing as well as a general definition was adopted as part of the Capotorti study, and reviewed in 1985, at the request of the Sub-Commission by Mr. Jules Deschênes.276 The working group on the draft declaration subsequently "agreed to postpone the consideration of the question of definition until a later stage," ie. until after a first reading of the substantive articles.277 However, both the Human Rights Committee, in applying Article 27, and the Committee on the Elimination of Racial Discrimination, have been able to examine the relevant aspects of State reports without the benefit of an explicit definition of "minority". It may also be noted that the term "peoples" which appears in the Charter and common article 1 of the two Covenants, is becoming generally accepted to include minorities or nationalities as it is being applied frequently in practice. The text of the Draft Declaration on which preliminary agreement has been reached so far reads as follows:

Draft declaration on the rights of persons belonging to national or ethnic, religious or linguistic minorities

The General Assembly,

Reaffirming that one of the basic aims of the United Nations, as proclaimed in its Charter, is to promote and encourage respect for human rights and for fundamental freedoms for all, without distinction as to race, sex, language or religion,

{Reaffirming} {Reiterating} {Declaring} faith in fundamental human rights, in the dignity and worth of the human person, in the equal rights of men and women and of nations large and small,

Desiring to promote the realization of the principles {concerning the rights of} {persons belonging to} {minorities} which form the basis of the

Charter of the United Nations, the Universal Declaration of Human Rights, the Convention on the Prevention and Punishment of the Crime of Genocide and the International Convention on the Elimination of All Forms of Racial Discrimination as well as other relevant international instruments {that have been adopted at the universal or regional level and those concluded between individual States Members of the United Nations},

Inspired by {Based on} the provisions of Article 27 of the International Covenant on Civil and Political Rights concerning the rights of persons belonging to ethnic, religious or linguistic minorities,

Considering that the promotion and protection of the rights of persons belonging to {national or} ethnic, religious or linguistic minorities contribute to the political and social stability of States in which they live,

Confirming that friendly relations and co-operation among States, which take place in the spirit of the Declaration on Principles of International Law concerning Friendly Relations and Co-operation among States in accordance with the Charter of the United Nations, contribute to international peace and security and to the creation of more favourable conditions for the realization and promotion of human rights, including the rights of {persons belonging to} {national or}, ethnic, linguistic and religious minorities,

Emphasizing that the constant promotion and realization of the rights of persons belonging to minorities, as an integral part of the development of society as a whole and within the constitutional framework, would in turn contribute to the strengthening of friendship and co-operation among peoples and States,

Bearing in mind the work done so far within the United Nations system, in particular the Commission on Human Rights, the Sub-Commission on Prevention of Discrimination and Protection of Minorities as well as the bodies established pursuant to the International Covenants on Human Rights and other relevant international human rights instruments on promoting and protecting the rights of persons belonging to {national or} ethnic, religious or linguistic minorities,

Recognizing the need to ensure even more effective implementation of international human rights instruments relating to the rights of persons belonging to {national or} ethnic, religious or linguistic minorities,

Proclaim this Declaration on the Rights of Persons Belonging to {National or} Ethnic, Religious or Linguistic Minorities:

Article 1

1. {Persons belonging to} {national or} ethnic, linguistic and religious minorities (hereinafter referred to as minorities) have the right to respect for, and the promotion of, their ethnic, cultural, linguistic and religious identity without any discrimination.
2. {Persons belonging to} minorities have the right to life, liberty and security of person and all other human rights and freedoms without discrimination.[278]

Historical Summary, USVCR

As we mentioned, the U.S. has no logically coordinated and officially expressed view of collective rights, having chosen instead the ideal of a fully assimilated society in which achieved non-discrimination will allow equal access of all members of her society to all the same processes and institutions of the system,[279] ie. the ideal of civil or individual rights. The ideal of equal justice before the law and the same rights for all is thought to be able to provide justice for minorities as well as for the majority.[280] However, as the preceding historical analysis revealed, U.S. society not only remains far from this ideal, it did not even countenance the idea of civil rights as extending to include its chief national minority until the period 1960-1975. The actual USVCR, therefore, had to be viewed within a longer historical perspective in order to be correctly interpreted and evaluated.

In the historical survey preceding, we note there were two post-slavery periods in the black minority's struggle from slavery towards equality in which its problems were given national attention and redress: the Reconstruction period following the Civil War, and the 1960-1975 riot period. In both these periods, marked by the minority's potential for vigorous and forceful self-assertion and by a menacing international environment, the American government hastily enacted reforms to palliate black demands, reforms which were either subsequently rescinded, or which proved ineffective in the ensuing quietus. In both periods, the reforms were in the immediate interests of the Anglo-American majority, and effectively disappeared when this was no longer so. We also saw that, during the interim apartheid period when the black minority pressure was at an ebb and the international environment most favorable to the security and well being of the U.S. majority,[281] the majority ethnicity chose to recognize from among emergent tendencies in the black community, only those groups or spokesmen whose objectives neither threatened majority interest nor involved any meaningful change in the status quo, conceptually or otherwise. As U.S. response to the problems of her chief national minority appeared to occur only at the behest of either international[282] and/or domestic pressure, and produce certain stop-gap measures rather than solutions from a comprehensive study of minority problems, we must deem the USVCR to be highly flexible and pragmatic .

Within this pragmatism, however, we can discern certain consistent elements or historical patterns:

* the tendency to interpret minority rights only in such a manner as to serve the interest of the majority ethnicity's economic and political needs; (this pattern or variable will be designated by the symbol MN, "majority needs")
* the tendency of the USVCR to adjust its formal apparatus for achieving majority economic and political needs, or dominance, to accord with the actual level of minority ethnic awareness expressed in terms of demands not capable of being quelled short of an unacceptable level of violence or civil disorder; (pattern or variable two will be designated by the symbol MD, "minority demands ")
* the ability of the USVCR to adjust domestic minority policies to suit the demands of a changing international environment in relation to the role the nation feels her national and economic wellbeing, plus transcendental values, demands; (variable three will be designated by the symbol IS, "international situation")
* of course, these three aspects of the USVCR's pragmatism required a consistent historical pattern of political and economic domination;283 (this constant will be designated by the symbol D, "domination ").

Thus, MN represents majority needs, MD represents minority demands, IS represents international environmental influence, and D represents domination. A fifth symbol (T) time, needs no prior clarification since all of the above variables and constant operate through time (T).

Using symbols borrowed from propositional logic, we may now formalize a general, functional, historically-based and politically descriptive definition of the USVCR:

$$\text{the USVCR} \equiv f(MN, MD, IS, T, D)$$

That is, that the USVCR, at any point in time, results from the interaction of MN, MD, IS, acting over time (T) and with domination (D), so as to maintain the majority interest (MI)284 as conceived by the Anglo-American ruling elites. Thus:

$$f(MN, MD, IS, T, D) = \frac{MN * MD * IS}{T*D} \Longleftrightarrow MI \text{ 285}$$

We have also said that assimilation (A) is the societal goal towards which the USVCR is said to be directed,286 and that minority equality or rights (MR) is said to result once this goal has been achieved.287

Therefore we may now write:

$$\text{USVCR} \equiv f(MN, MD, IS, T, D)$$
$$\text{also } f(MN, MD, IS, T, D) <=> M$$
$$\therefore MI ==> A$$
$$A ==> MR$$
$$\text{thus, } MI ==> MR$$

This notion that $MI ==> A ==> MR$ presupposes that either MR will always coincide with the pursuit of A and MI (which has been shown not to be the case in the U.S. historically as far as national minorities are concerned), or that MI must dominate MR and interpret MR in such a manner as will make it coincide with the pursuit of A and MI; thus, a key aspect of the USVCR becomes obvious: the fact that, in order for the USVCR to remain operational, the values of MR (minority rights) must not become a fixed universal (determined outside of U.S. domestic politics by international law, etc.). Returning again to our logical shorthand, we have by definition suggested that $MI ==> A$; $A ==> MR$ and that $MI <==> f \left(\dfrac{MN * MD * IS}{T * D} \right)$.

Therefore, it is this pragmatic function that must determine the values of

$$MR \left[f \left(\frac{MN * MD * IS}{T * D} \right) ==> MR \right].$$

At any point in time, MR must be able to change or be changed so that

$$\frac{f(MN * MD * IS)}{T * D}$$

will always also conform to MI. Any success at fixing or limiting the possible values of MR would render the USVCR inoperational because the USVCR is defined as being identical to

$$f \left(\frac{MN^* \ MD^* \ IS}{T^*D} \right) <==> MI.$$

In concluding, we will briefly demonstrate how the international law concept of collective rights in relation to national minorities must necessarily demarcate the possible values of the rights of national minority (MR) outside of the context of the function $\left(\dfrac{MR^* \ MD^* \ IS}{T^* \ D} \right)$ and in so doing, is fundamentally different from the U.S. approach to collective rights as it concerns national minorities (USVCR).

Differences Between the ILVCR and USVCR

The international law concept of collective rights, as it concerns national minorities, is significantly different from the USVCR in that it tends to universalize the definition of MR (outside of the needs of the U.S. majority interest). It calls for governments to officially (constitutionally and legally) recognize the minorities in their countries, and to provide for affirmative action or special measures whereby such minorities will be able to preserve their ethnic identity while entering into an equal-status relationship with the majority. The international law concept tends to discourage policies of Anglo-Saxonization under the guise of assimilation, in favor of pluralist policies. The following is a summary of the international law concepts relevant to defining or limiting the values of minority rights (MR).

Recognition and Special Measures or Affirmative Action

International human rights law envisages that the maintenance of ethnic identity and of adequate cultural development by minorities be achieved, first, by the minority's official (constitutional/legal) recognition by the state within which it is situated. A value of such recognition is that the minority so recognized is thus made eligible for the application of the provisions of international treaties or covenants concerning minorities which are presently in existence or which will be in the future.[288] Such recognition also makes permanent, rather than compensatory or provisional,[289] the concept of affirmative action or special measures to be summarized below. The USVCR, however, as we have shown in Part Two, provides no specific constitutional-legal recognition for its minorities; the USVCR legal approach to black minority problems through the means of civil rights acts, serves only to emphasize the needs for minority sameness with the majority, and overlooks its historical difference from the majority. It suggests that individuals can be equal without being the same; sameness is not a requirement for equality. Affirmative action must be undertaken to make minorities that are not the same, equal, and in their equal-status, they must have the right not to be the same.

Secondly, international human rights law envisages that state governments undertake to provide affirmative action or special measures, in order to ensure the equal status of their minorities, of their ethnic identities, and of their cultural development as desired. These special measures are measures *other* than those applied to the general population, measures which are applied to minorities by virtue of their being national minorities which are economically, politically or socially unequal. Equal status in relation to economic or cultural maintenance would require considerable human and financial resources; the right of persons belonging to a minority to preserve their own culture in economic equality with the majority would become entirely meaningless unless state governments provided assistance, for few if any national minorities have the means to guarantee their own economic, political or cultural survival.[290] This recognition by the ILVCR of governmental responsibility for minority protection and preservation is emphasized in the following statement by the Sub-Commission:

States are obliged not only to allow such measures (for cultural survival) to be pursued and to support them, but also to contribute by direct action to safeguarding the cultural values peculiar to minority groups in such a way that the numerical inferiority of the latter in relation to the rest of the population and a lack of resources do not lead to the extinction of those values. The objective to be attained is the preservation and natural development of the cultural identity of minorities. The State is therefore required to adopt all necessary measures to that end.[291]

The 1972 Helsinki International Conference on cultural policies in Europe reiterated and re-enforced this notion:

The right to culture implies a duty for governments and for the international community to make it possible for everyone, without distinction or discrimination of any kind, to take part in the cultural life of his community and of mankind in general.[292]

These special measures have, in short, two main functions: (a) to protect, preserve, and promote those distinctive aspects of minority culture, and (b) to promote the minority's equality of political and economic development and relationship with the majority ethny. The USVCR, however, as we have observed, officially provides for no affirmative actions or special measures for minority political and economic equality or for the preservation of minority culture.[293]

Finally, we must note that official recognition and affirmative action or special measures themselves act as elements which prevent the applicability of a policy of assimilation at any cost to the minority and without their knowing consent.

Pluralism vs. Assimilation

While international human rights law recognized the possibility that assimilation might be a desirable objective in (certain) multi-national countries, it does so always with the proviso that the minorities involved wished to assimilate:294

The objective of a policy of assimilation would be the establishment of a homogeneous society in which persons belonging to minority groups would have to abandon, even if gradually *but not forcibly* (emphasis added), their traditions, their culture and the use of their language in favour of the traditions, the culture and the language of the dominant group.295

Any assimilation which might take place must be clearly voluntary,296 and not at the price of the humiliation of the minority and the re-enforcement of a sense of inferiority on it. For a policy of assimilation to be voluntary, the minority concerned must both be advised that this goal is intended, and be queried for its consent. Such action should be supervised by a mutually agreed upon international organization.

However, while international law concedes the validity of an assimilationist policy in certain prescribed instances, the ILVCR strongly emphasizes the right of cultural identity, reminding multi-national states that the goal of abolishing discrimination against individuals, as embodied in the Universal Declaration of Human Rights, is inseparable from the problem of discrimination against ethnic groups. To this effect, the Sub-Commission states:

Many of the desires, needs and values of an individual arise from and are identified with a way of life characteristic of a group, and can be realized only through group activity. An undertaking to abolish discrimination against an individual if he becomes similar to the majority is obviously unsatisfactory in the case of those who do not seek to become completely like the majority.297

Thus, the ILVCR recommends pluralistic objectives for multi-national states such as the U.S.. U.N. document E/CN.4/Sub.2/384/Add. 5 explains that when minority groups are able to participate fully in the political, economic and social life of their country, and the richness and the contributions of their culture are recognized, they gain a sense of security which is indispensable for the elimination of inter-group tension.298

It is a widespread belief that if members of different groups come into contact with one another, friendlier attitudes will develop as a consequence. This is not always true. No amount of contact between (members of different groups) is likely to improve relations (in) cases (where) judgments of superiority or inferiority may merely be reinforced. What is needed is equal-status contact, in which the members of the ethnic groups which meet, represent comparable levels of position and prestige. Research has further indicated that contact has the best results when the two groups work together to achieve a common goal, particularly when success depends on co-operation.[299]

States should therefore undertake to combat the causes of inter-group antagonism and adopt concrete affirmative action measures designed to promote equal understanding, co-operation and harmonious equal-status relations. However, the elimination of tension and friction cannot be achieved if the realities of cultural, religious and linguistic differences between the various components of the society are not taken into account. "Experience shows that in a multi-national society, the most effective way to build a just, peaceful and united nation, is for the state concerned to adopt a policy which allows members of ethnic, religious and linguistic groups to *preserve their own characteristics* (emphasis added)." [300]

We may now conclude that the USVCR is significantly different from the international law concept of collective rights in relation to national minorities as expressed in the legal principles of Article 27. The USVCR does not yet encompass the constitutional-legal recognition of the existence of its national minorities or accept to officially provide affirmative action or special measures for their political and economic equality and cultural development or the ratification of the major human rights treaties which may in effect increase domestic pressure for affirmative action or special measures and recognition. The acceptance of the international law view by the government of the U.S. would not only serve to render the present USVCR inoperative, but would also substantially alter the current societal objectives regarding the rights and future of America's national minorities. Were the option of choice between the two concepts to be made open to the chief U.S. national minorities under the supervision of an international organization, we believe that a substantial body of opinion would emerge from within the black minority and other national minorities, in support of affirmative action and perhaps of a non-assimilationist, pluralistic option as propounded in international human rights law.[301]

The question of whether such a choice will ever be made available to U.S. national minorities depends on how the U.S. actually views its national minorities, and should provide a key to answering the subjective question of whether the U.S. minority concept, the

USVCR, is just out of step with international law, or is in reality a system of domestic colonialism and internal imperialism (evolving as it does from intentional enslavement, extermination and gross exploitation) that had and has no intention of providing its national minorities with their universally accepted human rights as national minorities, nor of permitting them to become aware of such rights, or of themselves as a people who may require, for equal status, at least some form of self-determination. The continuous failure of the U.S. government to recognize these basic facts and internationally protected minority rights is likely to eventually lead to an internationally-supported struggle for some form of self-determination. Such a struggle for self-determination would of necessity resemble the many national liberation struggles that have been causing so much difficulty for world peace.

The essence of the problem was captured in the words of Richard Falk of Princeton University, when he wrote:

> We need to understand the extent to which there exists in all parts of the world now, an awareness that one of the great current problems of world order, is the plight of what I would call entrapped nations, nations that are entrapped within the structure and framework of the sovereign state. An enormous juristic fraud has been perpetrated on modern political consciousness by confusing national identity with the power political reality of state sovereignty. The whole idea of what ie means to be a national has been converted through a formal juristic device into a legal status that the state confers, which, for the majority of people living in the world, does not correspond with their ethnic, psychological and political reality. Their sense of what it means to belong to a collectivity, however one describes it, whether in tribal terms or in national terms, is often at odds with a network of imposed obligations owed to the sovereign state. Rather than a sense of loyalty associated with the natural sentiment of nationality, there exists a condition of political alienation in a variety of forms.302

The significance for domestic peace and order, from the viewpoint of those nations Falk sees as entrapped, can perhaps best be stated by paraphrasing the words of an early western philosopher, Jean-Jacques Rousseau:

> It can be said that the government does not provide for the human rights of self-determination for American minorities because to do so would be too expensive and may disrupt law and order. But what good is this domestic peace or 'enforced order' to American minorities living in a state of gross inequality and injury. What advantage is it, if this law, order and peace itself is

based on American minorities agreeing to be contented with poverty and oppression? If this peace is in fact one of their miseries? One can have law and order while living in a jail. The Greeks, while enclosed in the cage of the Cyclops, lived in peace while waiting to be eaten.*

*{On dira que le depote assure a ses sujets le tranquillité civile. Ou' y gagnent-ils, a cette tranquillité même est une de leurs misères? On vit tranquille aussi dans les cachets. Les grecs enfermeés dans l'antre du cyclope y vivoient tranquilles, en attendent que leur tour vint d'être dévores.}303

APPENDIX I

In writing this book, I sought opinions from a number of experienced people or their writings and I list them here to thank them for their time and as a useful resource list for those who seek further readings or contacts.

ABZUG, Bella, Congresswoman, Statement concerning Human Rights in the Philippines, Oct. 11, 1973.

ALDRICH, George, H., Acting Legal Advisor, Department of State.

BACON, Ruth, Director, U.S. Center for International Women's Year, 1975.

BITKER, Bruno, former U.S. representative to the United Nations International Conference on Human Rights.

BRESLIN, Patrick, Project Director, Humanitarian Policy Studies Program, Carnegie Endowment for International Peace, Washington, D.C.

BRUE, Cameron, Legislative Representative, Americans for Democratic Action, Washington, D.C.

BUCKLEY, William Jr., Editor, *National Review*

BUERGENTHAL, Thomas, Professor of Law, State University of New York, Buffalo.

CAHIER, Ph., Professor at the Graduate Institute of International Studies, Geneva.

CARTER, Jimmy, ex-President of the United States, see in particular his address to the United Nations.

CHRISTOPHER, Warren, Deputy Secretary of State.

CLARKE, Ramsey, Former Attorney General of the United States.

COHEN, Herman J. Director, Office of Central African Affairs, U.S. Department of State.

CONSTABLE, Peter, Director of Pakistani and Bangladesh Affairs, U.S. Department of State.

CROWLEY, Harriet, Deputy Assistant Administrator, Bureau for Population and Humanitarian Assistance, A.I.D.

DEARDEN, Cardinal John, Archbishop of Detroit, Michigan.

DERIAN, Patricia, Coordinator-Designator of Human Rights and Humanitarian Affairs, Department of State.

DOBRIONSKEY, Dr. Lev. E., Professor of Georgetown University, President, Ukrainian Congress Committee of America, Chairman, National Captive Nations Committee.

ENNALS, Martin, Secretary General, Amnesty International.

FALK, Richard, Professor of International Law, Center of International Studies, Princeton University.

FARER, Tom S., Professor of Law, Rutgers University.

FELDMAN, D., Professor at the University of Kazan, U.S.S.R.

FOX, Donald T., see in particular documents from the American Society of International Law.

FRASER, Arvonne S., President, Women's Equity Action League.

FRASER, Donald, see in particular *Foreign Policy Magazine,* Spring, 1977

GAREY, John, Alternative U.S. member, U.N. Sub-Commission on Prevention of Discrimination and Protection of Minorities.

GOLDBERG, Arthur J., Chairman of the Ad hoc Committee on the Human Rights and Genocide Treaties.

HANSELL, Herbert J., Legal Advisor, Secretary of State.

HENDSCH, Shirley B., Bureau of International Affairs, Department of State.

HENKIN, Louis, Professor of International Law, Columbia University Law School .

HERNDL, K., Assistant Secretary-General for Human Rights, United Nations.

HESBURGH, Theodore, President, Notre Dame University.

HEWITT, Warren, Bureau of International Organization Affairs, Department of State.

HOFFMA N, Philip, U .S. Representative to the United Nations Commission on Human Rights.

HUMPHREY, John, Former Director, United Nations Division of Human Rights.

JACK, Homer A., Secretary-General, World Conference of Religion for Peace .

JENNINGS, James, Associate Director, U.S. Catholic Conference, Division of Justice and Peace.

JENKINS, Kempton B., Deputy Assistant Secretary of State for Congressional Relations, Department of State.

JESSUP, Philip C., Former Judge, International Court of Justice.

KENNEDY, Edward A., U.S. Senator from Massachusetts.

KEYS, Donald Freaser, United Nations Representative for the World Federalists.

KOREY, William, See in particular *World Magazine,* September, 1972.

LACHS, H.E.M., Judge and former President of the International Court of Justice, Member of the International Law Institute.

LANDIS, Elizabeth, American Committee on Africa.

LISKOFSKY, Sidney, American Jewish Committee.

LOW, Stephen, Country Director for Brazil, Department of State.

MACDERMOT, Niall, Secretary-General of the International Commission of Jurists.

MAHMOUD, Dr. M.A., Director, International Center of Legal Science, The Hague.

MAYMI, Carmen, Director, Women's Bureau, U.S. Department of Labor.

McMANUS, Frank, Member of the House of Commons, United Kingdom.

MEANY, George, President, AFL-C10.

MORRIS, Roger, Carnegie Endowment for International Peace.

NEWMAN, Frank, Professor, School of Law, University of California, Berkeley .

O'BRADAIGH, Ruairi, President, Sinn Fein, Ireland.

O'BRIEN, Fred Burns, "British Violations of the Human Rights Declaration", 1973.

POPPER, David, H., Assistant Secretary, Bureau of Organization Affairs, Department of State.

PROXMIRE, William, U.S. Senator from Wisconsin.

PR U GN, Maj or General George S., The Judge Advocate-General, U.S. A rmy.

QUIGLEY, Thomas, U.S. Catholic Conference, Latin America Bureau.

REID, Ogden, Congressional Representative, New York.

RITTENHOUSE, Stanley, E., Legislative Aide, Liberty Lobby, Washington, D.C.

SCHWEIG, Egon, Professor Emertius, Yale Law School.

SHESTACK, Jerome J., Chairman, International League for the Rights of Man.

SNYDER, Edward F., Friends Committee on National Legislation, Washington, D.C.

TINKER, Irene, Federation of Organizations for Professional Women.

WALKER, Julius, Director of Regional Affairs, Bureau of African Affairs, Department of State.

WEISSBRODT, David, Associate Professor, University of Minnesota Law School, Minneapolis.

WERTSMAN, Bernard G., Article "The Rest of the World Sees Them Differently", *New York Times,* March 6, 1977.

WOETZEL, Robert, Professor, International Politics and Law, Boston College.

WRIGHT, Marshall, Assistant Secretary for Congressional Relations.

ZIMMERMAN, Maud Ellen, Voters' Interests League, Baltimore, Maryland.

APPENDIX II
A POLITICAL VIEW OF IMMIGRANT AND
SUB-GROUP MINORITIES

Apart from the legal study of state papers, treaties, and the historical practice of civilized nations, interviews at the Ottawa and Washington embassies of the major European nations revealed that when nation-states speak of minority rights as defined in Article 27, they are referring usually to national, linguistic, ethnic and religious minorities (LERMs). Immigrant LERMs were generally spoken of in the sense of helping them to assimilate into the predominant culture of the region in which they had chosen to live. Indeed, states appeared to take for granted the idea that anyone wishing to immigrate expected to assimilate. Sub-group minorities were generally not seen as being different from the ethny with which they were associated. When sub-group minorities were mentioned, most state representatives would appear somewhat surprised, and respond to the effect that the group mentioned was a part of the major ethny and thus shared the same rights and freedoms. Following are what we found to be typical examples of immigrant LERMs and sub-group minorities.

Sub-Group Minorities

As mentioned in the Introduction, we construed this term to refer to groups which identify and are identified completely with the majority ethny, but which also have certain differences that are not ethnic, religious or linguistic, which set them apart to a significant degree from other members of the majority, ie. belonging to a particular political party, a certain class, etc.. In general, such groups are not recognized as minorities in International Human Rights Law although they may be non-dominant sociologically and numerically.[304] The protection of such sub-group minorities generally falls under the general instruments of individual human rights protection, although special categories of such groups are sometimes recognized by special convention, etc..[305]

An excellent example of the sub-group type of minority can be seen in the Dowa of Japan. Officially, Japan claims to be a nation-state containing a single Japanese race or ethny. The constitution outlaws all forms of discrimination based on sex, creed, race, social status or family origin; however, it is officially recognized that on the level of the peoples' daily life there actually exists a segment of people (sub-group minority) who in reality are not fully guaranteed fundamental human rights, nor enjoy full civil rights and liberties. This sub-group minority situation is known as the "Dowa" problem.

The Dowa are a segment of the Japanese peoples who, because of discrimination based on a class system formed in the process of the historical development of Japanese society, are placed in such an inferior position economically, socially and culturally, that their fundamental human rights are grossly violated. These peoples live together in particular districts and form separate communities within these districts. Recently, many Dowa have attempted to leave these particular districts to live in ordinary areas, but because of their birth in the traditionally separated communities, they are subject to social discrimination. In ancient Japan, the Dowa were known as "Tokushu Buraku" or "Korhin Buraka" (backward communities) and "Saimin Buraku" (indigent communities). Today they are popularly called "Mikaiho Buraka (unliberated communities). Although various sociological and anthropological theories attribute the Dowa origins to ethnic, religious, occupational and/or political causation, in modern political terminology, it appears that the Dowa problem resulted from uneven societal development, where imperialistic feudal societies moving towards capitalistic development have experienced societal disarticulation in the emergence of the so-called traditional and modern sectors. This is suggested by the more official theory, which states that around the outset of the 17th century during the Tokugawa reign, the Dowa class was restricted by political, economic and social conditions of the feudal society, and was settled in particular districts. These residents during the feudal period were defined as humble peoples of the lowest rank (similar to serfdom in Europe). At the time of the Meiji regime (the Meiji restoration is credited by political scientists with beginning the construction of modern industrial Japan) in 1868, a cabinet ordinance No. 61 formally emancipated the Dowa from their legal feudal status.

In 1935, the government mapped out a 10 year 'integration' plan, but it was not completed because Japan entered a long period of war preparation. After the war, special measures for Dowa districts were temporarily suspended because of the administration policy of the allied occupation forces. After the coming into force of the peace treaty of 1952, the Japanese government established subsidies for the establishment of public facilities for counselling and other services in the Dowa districts. Late in 1958, the ministerial conference on the Dowa problem was established. In 1966, the Prime Minister's office established the Dowa policy consultative council to help solve the Dowa problem, and in 1969, the government enacted the law on special measures for Dowa projects and mapped out a long-term policy program. The law of special measures which will be effective until 1979 attempts to eliminate those factors which unduly obstruct the improvement of the social and economic position of Dowa. Both local and national governments are asked to promote and carry out these measures in a systematic manner. In 1969, the total appropriation for Dowa districts stood at $6,200 millions. This total has expanded each year, reaching 7,139,200 in fiscal 1977. The number of projects subsidized by the Japanese government in 1969 were 13. The present total is 53. In spite of direct involvement by the Japanese government, the problem of the Dowa minority still remains to be eliminated. If the problem is indeed one of societal disarticulation as suggested, it is likely that the problem is connected to the mode of production in the Japanese highly capitalistic economic system.

This Japanese example of a sub-group contains several points that may be useful when considering the sub-group classification:

1. The Dowa minority is considered as a sub-group of the dominant Japanese ethny and identifies completely with the majority ethny
2. The sub-group is based on characteristics considered undesirable both by the sub-group and the other Japanese.
3. The long-term objective of the Japanese government is the elimination of this sub-group.
4. Special government constitutional and legal structures were temporarily created to achieve this purpose and to assimilate sub-group members into the larger Japanese society with which it is said to completely identify.

Immigrant Minorities

United Nations Minority Rights Law does not distinguish between national and immigrant minorities; thus both are accorded the same rights. Article 27 of the Covenant of Civil and Political Rights applies equally to this category as it does to national minorities. However, this group consists of individuals who leave their native country and emigrate to another country after the peoples of that country and its international existence has been formally recognized. We have stated that we feel, for important political reasons, that this type of minority has protection needs different from those of national minorities and should not be automatically considered for the purposes of minority protection under Article 27 as before mentioned. Several members of the Sub-Commission also expressed the opinion that individuals usually emigrate to a country and become citizens of a country other than their own, with the implicit, if not voiced, intention to assimilate into the society of the existing national ethnies of that country. Also, countries often accept immigrants with this implicit or explicit understanding. To ignore such an understanding and to extend 'carte blanche' collective rights under Article 27 to immigrant minorities on the same basis as national minorities may have the effect of seriously crippling the willingness and capability of certain nations to accept immigrants, and/or their willingness to ratify human rights treaties which include minority protection devices. Countries such as the U.S., whose population was produced largely through the assimilation of more than thirty-five million European immigrants,[283] are no doubt more reluctant to accept Article 27 because it applies also to immigrant minorities; while this view is not the focus of this research, we do feel that the continuous existence to an uncertain degree of self-consciousness among certain immigrant minorities such as the Italians, Poles, etc., may also be a factor influencing the reluctance of the Senate to ratify the major human rights treaties. This is probably true although U.S. immigrants seem relatively content with the idea of individual human rights. It is the lack of collective rights for national minorities that poses the significant threat to peaceful relations among and within states; thus, it would be unfortunate if the United Nations attitude of extending the same type of rights to all minorities served to justify the non-compliance of states with the requirements of Article 27, as it concerns national minorities; or to excite into action elements of immigrant population which otherwise would be content with assimilation.

Indeed, the traditional attitude of countries has been one of assimilation with various special considerations in relation to immigrant minorities, and should minority protection be developed within the framework of the principles of international law, it will eventually make some distinction between the rights of immigrant and national minorities. [307]

France offers an example of the traditional attitude of countries toward the assimilation of immigrant minorities. Discussions at the French Embassy revealed that France, similar to Japan, constitutionally-legally defined itself as consisting of a single ethny or race, an ethny or race which is willing to extend itself to include assimilated immigrants.[308] However, the Sub-Commission and the occasional acts by nationalists in Bretagne, as well as the increasing discrimination against and exclusion of North Africans from acceptance in French society call this view into question.

Some statistics, however, reflect the importance of the high degree of French immigrant minority assimilation. In 1973, out of a total of 400,000 marriages, 27,500 were marriages in which one of the spouses belonged to an immigrant minority. In addition, 85,000 of the 730,000 births in France in 1974 included children of which one parent was a member of an immigrant minority. Although 59% of all immigrants live in the industrial regions of Paris, the Rhone, the Alps, Provence and the Riviera, 22.9% of the population of Corsica is composed of immigrant minorities. Although the immigrant minorities in France make up the most significant minority segment as far as numbers are concerned, in France as in most other multi-national states, it is the national minorities of Breton, Corsica and Alsace that pose the most significant minority demands. The immigrant minority problem consists of finding methods of integrating this minority into the mainstream of French society, of avoiding the economic exploitation of immigrants, and of absorbing the cultural shock to French traditions. The latter problem should be made more acceptable by the fact that France's immigrant minorities come mostly from Latin, Francophone and Mediterranean countries: Portugal, Italy, Spain, Morocco, Algeria, Tunisia, plus some from Poland and Yugoslavia. Algeria, Morocco and Tunisia were former French colonies whose members already shared many of the French cultural traditions. Spain, Italy and Portugal share many of the same Latin traditions as France, while the Poles and Yugoslavs account for only a small proportion of the immigrant minorities: 86,408 and 77,810 respectively. Algerians, who have a special legal status in France, account for the largest immigrant population with 884,320,[309] followed by the Portuguese with 858,929. It is this large Algerian population with Islamic traditions and customs quite different from the French, that has posed the chief problem regarding assimilation. However, like immigrant minorities in other countries, their main objectives are either assimilation into the French nation or the achievement of economic benefit and a return to Algeria, or both. The French civil law provided for religious freedom, so although their Islamic background may serve as a blockage to their quick assimilation, demand for religious or cultural freedom was never an issue during this writer's period of observation (1972-1985). To meet the needs of its large immigrant minorities, the French government despite the general increase in racism has concentrated its attention on formal and special status, constitutional and legal guarantees providing rights and services which these minorities will need. Also, the French government has established such government structures as: l'Office national d'immigration, le Fonds d'action sociale, le Service social d'aide aux emigrants, l'Association pour l'enseignement des etrangers, etc..

REFERENCES

1 François Perroux in his work *Indépendance de l'économie nationale et inerdépendance des nations,* Aubier Montaigne, Paris, 1969 shows that, due to economic and political necessity, each state seeks its national interest in its international relations. Benjamin J. Cohen in *The Question of Imperialism,* Basic Books Inc., New York, 1973 demonstrates that such is the case because of the anarchic nature of the international system. This writer sees these factors as causing the chief differences that exist between international law and national law: namely, international law is primarily accepted or adhered to because it is conceived of as being in the long term self interest of the nation-state. Apparently no nation-state accepts or adheres to a rule or principle in international law when the comparative short term and long term results are considered more harmful than useful to its national interest. In the book *Rio, Reshaping the International Order,* a report to the Club de Rome, Anthony J. Dolman, Editor, Jan Van Ettinger, Director, 1977, Professor Jan Tinbergen points out why international law is one factor necessary for long term human survival and progress.

2 Wesley L. Gould and Michael Barkun, *International Law and the Social Sciences,* Princeton University Press, Princeton, N.J., 1970 (Chapter VI - International Procedurse). In Chapter VI, the authors speak about the intermingling of law and bargaining. Many scholars express the opinion that international law represents to a significant degree, important aspects of world opinion. Curtis Arthur Amlund, "Towards the Establishment of World Law: from Possibility to Probability," *Southwestern Science Quarterly,* Vol. 46, December 1965, pp. 281-288; M.J. Hendry, "Ethics, Values and the Common Good as Guidelines for a World Community," *Ottawa Law Review,* Vol. 74, April 1976, pp. 865-892. Also a comparison of the following U.N. statements on individual rights under international law of 1948 to 1971 will indicate the degree to which individuals and groups within nations are increasingly becoming the subject of international law. For statements see U.N. Doc. E/CN.4/1 (November 5, 1948); U.N. Publ. 1948 v. 1; and U.N. Doc. E/CN.4/245 (April 28, 1971), pp. 195--204.

3 Conflicts arising from the laws of the sea, of the air, etc. are often successfully handled through the use of international law. See Wolfgang Friedmann, Oliver J. Lissitzyn and Richard C. Pugh, *International Law: Cases and Materials,* West Publishing Co., St. Paul, Minnesota, 1969, pp. 243-258.

4 U.N. Doc. E/CN.4/Sub 2/384/Add. 1, page 25.

5 The recent Greek-Turkish conflict in Cyprus is an example of minority-majority conflicts which might have led to war between involved nations and their allies.

6 Joseph B. Kelly, "National Minorities in International Law," *Denver Journal of International Law and Policy,* Vol. 3, No. 2, Fall 1973, pp. 253-73. Also, in the statement of Herman J. Cohen, Director, Office of Central African Affairs, U.S. Department of State, attention was called to the case of Burundi. There, two tribes which probably never could have agreed to become members of the same nation-state, had it not been for the colonial past, were in mortal conflict, which to date has claimed more than 100,000 lives of the Hutu tribe, and led the U.N. to raise the

charge of genocide against the Tutsi tribe which composes the government. See Hearings befor the U.S. Sub-Committee of International Organizations and Movements, August 1, 1973, p. 70.

7 Here we refer to such conflicts as: Québeçois and Aboriginal Peoples (Canada); Scottish, Irish, Welsh (Great Britain); Chicanos, Indians, Eskimos, Blacks (U.S.); Basques, Catalans (Spain). It is significant to note that while the conflicts and the potential for minority conflicts exist in Europe, Canada and the U.S., most minorities in advanced Western nations live in relative peace and equality with their national majorities. Elaborate minority protection machinery has developed in these countries, particularly in Europe and Canada. For examples of such machinery, see "Patterns of Future Government," Her Majesty's Stationery Office, Northern Ireland Office, 1975, part 3, p. 10. Also Belgium, Norway, Sweden, Greece and Switzerland are examples of countries in which minorities have lived in relative peace and equality over long periods of time.

8 J. Claydon, "The Transnational Protection of Ethnic Minorities: A Tentative Framework for Enquiry", *The Canadian Yearbook of International Law,* Vol. XIII, 1975, pp. 25-60.

9 Yoram Dinstein, "Collective Human Rights of Peoples and Minorities", *The International and Comparative Law Quarterly,* Vol. 25, Part 1, January 1976, pp. 102-20.

10 Rita Hauser, "International Protection of Minorities and the Right of Self- Determination", *Israel Yearbook on Human Rights,* Vol. 92, 1971.

11 Claude L. Inis, *National Minorities, an International Problem,* Greenwood Press, New York, 1969.

12 Kelly, *loc. cit.*

13 For all political and legal purposes, without self-awareness there would be no minority. This is the subjective element.

14 Ernest Baker, *National Character and the Factors in its Formations,* Methuen and Co., London, 1948, p. 247.

15 Felix Maurice Hippisley, *Napoleon and the Awakening of Europe,* Collier Books, New York, 1965.

16 Belgium offers a case in point. In 1830, the Walloons and Flemish peoples of Belgium rose up against what they both perceived as unacceptable rule by the alien Dutch. But rather than develop separate states, the two nations not only elected to remain in a single state, but to offer the Belgian crown to a royal heir of France, and then to a German prince. See John Emerich Edward Dalberg-Acton, *The History of Freedom and Other Essays,* Books for Libraries Press, New York, 1967, p. 284.

17 Although Marx was an internationalist, he recognized the strategic and moral value of aligning the communist movement with national aspirations. The term 'right of self-determination' appeared for the first time in the Marxist Proclamation on the Polish Question.

18 The Wilsonian application of the doctrine concerned minorities of the Austrian-Hungarian, German and Ottoman empires, and certain peoples who would otherwise be part of the U.S.S.R.. See M. Pomerance, "U.S. and Self-Determination: Perspective on the Wilsonian Conception", *American Journal of International Law,* Vol. 70, January 1976, pp. 1-27.

19 " L'Amerique, rnaitre du monde," Chapter 11, report to the Club de Rome, lecture notes (Les theories du developpement), Professor Jorge Aviles, Université Laval, trimestre d'automne 1974, p. 29.

20 Louis Henkin, "International Organization and the Rule of Law", *International Organization,* Vol. XXIII, No. 3, Summer 1969, pp. 656-679.

21 While such scholars as Professor J. Claydon, *op cit.*, and Professor J.B. Kelly, *op. cit.*, show how the U.S. influences work against emphasizing minority rights in the U.N., this same U.S. emphasis can be abstracted from her predominant role in the Organization of American States. As to the rights to be enjoyed by alien minorities living in the American Republics, the Eighth Conference cast its Resolution XXVII in terms suggesting that it was disclaiming the treaty system of protecting minority groups that had been employed in Europe following World War 1. Postulating that the conditions characterizing the groups known as minorities do not exist in America, the resolution declares that 'residents who, according to domestic law are considered aliens, cannot claim collectively the condition of minorities; individually, however, they will continue to enjoy the rights to which they are entitled'. Louis Sohn and Thomas Buergenthal, *Basic Documents on International Protection of Human Rights*, Bobbs-Merrill, New York, 1973.

22 There is no reason to assume that the U.S. melting pot in relation to immigrant European minorities and apartheid politics in relation to its black minorities would not influence the type of international concepts it wishes to be surrounded by. Indeed, we suggest a logical connection between the type of human rights emphasized by the U.S. and her minority problem.

23 The Soviet system (opposite of the U.S.), has often been attacked by the U.S. on charges of violation of individual rights. Such charges are historically well known. However, the problem encountered by Jewish and other individuals seeking the right to leave the U.S.S.R. or to publically express individual non-communist opinions seems the result rather of an effort to establish socialism and a classless society.

24 It is interesting to note that the minorities in the U.S.S.R. were organized and integrated into the U.S.S.R. under the banner of national self-determination and communism. In an interview at Cornell University Law School, June 1978, with Professor Boris Topornin, Head of the sector on constitutional and governmental law of the U.S.S.R., it was repeatedly emphasized that without this orientation, the U.S.S.R. may not have been able to peacefully unite its minorities into a multinational state. Thus, the historic roots of national minorities in the U.S.S.R. results from compromises for nation building, while as before mentioned, national minorities in the U.S. result from the slave trade and the acquisition of territory by the ancient right of conquest.

25 Georg Schwarzenberger and George W. Keeton, *The Inductive Approach to International Law*, Stevens and Sons, London, 1965. Also see Wolfgang Friedmann, Oliver J. Lissitzyn and Richard C. Pugh, *International Law: Cases and Materials*, West Publishing Co., St. Paul, Minnesota, 1969, pp. 11-33.

26 Transcripts of U.N. proceedings particularly point to the U.S. and United Kingdom as attempting to de-emphasize collective rights. See Kelly, *op. cit.*, p. 266. Domestically the U.S.S.R. is organized in accordance with the principle of emphasizing collective rights in relation to minorities, while the U.S. and United Kirgdom are not. U.S.S.R. foreign policy advocating decolonization is in line with its collective rights emphasis, while the western powers, who had colonies, claimed instead that their colonial inhabitants were citizens with 'the same rights' as citizens of the mother country - a conceptualization that emphasizes individual rights while allowing for exploitation and domination.

27 S.K. Jha, "The United Nations and Human Rights", *India Quarterly*, Vol. 29, July-September 1973, pp. 239-249.

28 Andrew Martin, "Human Rights and World Politics", *Yearbook of World Affairs*, Vol. 5, 1951, pp. 37-80.

29 M. Pomerance, 'The U.S. and Self-Determination: Perspectives on the Wilsonian Conception", *American, Journal of International Law,* Vol. 70, 1976, pp. 1-27. See also Morton A. Kaplan, *The Rationale for NATO,* American Institute for Public Policy Research, Washington, D.C., 1973.

30 Hans Gruber, "Human Rights- Important Agenda Item of the XXVIIth U.N. General Assembly", *Human Rights,* 1973, p. 438.

31 The U.S.S.R.'s support for these resolutions is reported in the *Basic Documents on International Protection of Human Rights,* Bobbs-Merrill, New York, 1973, by Louis Sohn and Thomas Buergenthal.

32 E.E. Kudryavtsev, "Truth About Human Rights", *Human Rights,* Vol. 5, Winter 1976 pp. 193-99. This article explores the details of the above-mentioned gap.

33 Louis Henkin, "International Organization and the Rule of Law", *International Organization,* Vol. XXIII, No. 3, Summer 1969, pp. 656-79. While the record of the U.S.S.R. is somewhat better than the U.S. as far as ratification of the major human rights treaties, the U.S.S.R. has only ratified three of the major human rights treaties of concern to this research. Also due to the lack of individual civil and political freedoms in the U.S.S.R. (as we know them in the West), it is doubtful to what degree the economic and collective rights stressed by the U.S.S.R. can be actually practiced in the U.S.S.R.. Although this factor should be mentioned, we will not deal with it in this research. Our emphasis is on the U.S. and international law concepts of collective rights as it concerns minorities.

34 From this point forward, USHRFP will occasionally be used to represent 'the credibility of the U.S. human rights foreign policy.'

35 From this point forward, USVCR and ILVCR will be used to represent the definitions as defined above.

36 See S.P. Sinha, 'Is Self-Determination Passé?", *Colurrbia Journal of Transnational Law,* Vol. 12, 1973, pp. 260-73. In this article, Sinha suggests that the right of self-determination is being denied the black American, the Irish Catholics in Northern Ireland, and the French Canadian. Also see Nayar Kaladharan, "Self-Determination Beyond the Colonial Context", *Texas International Law Journal,* Vol. 10, Spring 1975, pp. 321-45; Thomas M. Franck and Paul Offman, "The Right of Self-Determination in Very Small Places", *New York Journal of International Law and Politics,* Vol. 8, No. 2, Winter 1976, p. 331; J. Claydon, "The Transnational Protection of Ethnic Minorities", *op. cit.,* pp. 25-60.

37 Pierre Vallieres, *Les nègres blancs d'Amérique,* Parti Pris, Montreal, 1968. While a student at the University of Montreal (1968-70), this writer could clearly discern the impact of this interpretation from popular reaction.

38 Northern Ireland Discussion Paper 3, *The Government of Northern Ireland,* Northern Ireland Office, HMS0, pp. 3-27.

39 See AFP-Moscow, "L'U.R.S.S. dénonce le rapport Carter", *Le Devoir,* June 8, 1977; Reuter-Havana, ""Etats-Unis - Cuba, echange de dipl8mates au lieu des insultes", *Le Soleil,* June 20, 1977; Graham Hovey, "U.S. Faces Challenge on Puerto Rico at U.N." *N.Y. Times,* August 20, 1977; Tom Wicker, "The New South and the Old", *N.Y. Times,* p. C35, August 16, 1977, Wayne King, "Bond Accuses Carter of Ignoring Blacks", *N.Y. Times,* August 16, 1977, p. C16.

40 CBS 19:OO o'clock T.V. News, March 7th, 1977. See also Nations Unies, Reuters and AFP, "Les Droits de l'homme ne sont pas une affaire interieur", *Le Devoir,* March 18, 1977; Reuter-AFP Belgrade, "Pour permettre un large debat sur les droits de l'homme", *Le Devoir,* June 2, 1977; AFP Washington, "Carter paraph le pacte de San Jose", *Le Devoir,* June 18, 1977; Bernard Brigouleix, "Carter, espoir des dissidents Sovietiques", *Le Devoir,* June 14, 1977; Kathleen Teltsch, "Young,

in Costa Rica Backs Rights Grive", *N.Y. Times,* August 10, 1977; Graham Hovey, "U.S. Quietly Protested Jailing of Reporters in Central African Empire", *N.Y. Times,* August 17,

41 As noted by Professor Kelly, *op. cit.,* pp. 264-65, "... it is most significant that the concept of assimilation was predominant in the development of the post-war international system. In this regard, the role of the U.S. is of the utmost importance... The League Minorities System had, of course, developed without any input from the U.S.... In 1945, however, the U.S. was not only present, but dominant... the assimilationist attitude was very popular in both the U.S. and Great Britain... The Western attitude was hardened in this respect by the pro-minorities view expounded by the Soviet Union..."

42 On this point, Henkin, *op. cit.,* p. 669, goes so far as to state: 'in regard to law at least as much as elsewhere, what international organization had done and not done is in substantial measure due to the United States, to its preeminent contribution in money, personnel, ideas and initiatives, as well as to its restraints. The policies of the United States, however, have not been uniform... nor, of course, have they always and completely prevailed. "Also the first part of this section dealt with this suggestion.

43 As Professor Kelly noted: "Minority protection and U.S. assimilation are manifestly incompatible." Kelly, *op. cit.,* p. 264. Also see earlier discussion on the U.S. policy in the United Nations and conclusion to Part Two.

44 Professor S.K. Jha denotes this same point. "The Commission of Human Rights started the work of drafting the covenants in 1947. But in the beginning itself there developed a controversy between the western democracies and the socialist states; the former wanted a covenant on human rights in the context of basic civil rights, while the latter put stress on collective and economic rights". S.K. Jha, "The United Nations and Human Rights", *India Quarterly,* Vol. 29, July-September 1973, p. 239.

45 While we found less emphasis on the right to own private property in the new initiative, we do not feel that this is significant to our research because the unpopularity of U.S. ownership in other countries would lead to the logical tactical de-emphasis of this right. Also we read nothing to indicate that the U.S. traditional ideas on private ownership had changed.

46 U.N. Doc.E/CN-4/376/l950

47 For example, U.N. Doc. E/CN.4/Sub.2/L 582 (1973); U.N. Doc. E/C/CN.4/Sub.2/L. 595 (1974); U.N. Doc. E/CN.4/Sub.2/L. 621 (1975).

48 While the Sub-Commission held discussions on the various types of minorities mentioned, the human rights minority law is cased in general terms which apply equally to any group having the status of the legal minority. However, during discussions in the Sub-Commission each of these types of minorities is often spoken of in separate fashions, indicating the expectation of different types of demands and needs. For example, in speaking about immigrant minorities, emphasis is placed on the right to equal protection before the law, etc.. Thus, the U.N. Sub-Commission in applying "*Jus aquum*" to the question of minorities may have overlooked important treatment distinctions. In this research, we have accepted the actual ILVCR providing equal protection to all official minorities, but have decided to deal with only one of the types of minorities recognized in the ILVCR.

49 See U.N. Doc. E/CN.4/Sub.2/L. 582, June 1973; U.N. Doc. E/CN.4/Sub.2/L. 595, July 1974; U.N. Doc. E/CN.4/Sub.2/L. 621, July 1975.

50 After discussion on the subgroup type of minorities, the Sub-Commission decided not to consider such groups (e.g. political groups) as eligible for minority protection, while immigrant minorities were afforded protection.

51 Most of the scholars mentioned in Part Two viewed the black minority as a U.S. minority. Few expressed the view that the black minority could be considered a black segment of the Anglo-American population.

52 In this quotation by Bell, ("Racial Remediation: a Historical Perspective on Current Conditions", *Notre Darne Lawyer*, Vol. 52:5, October 1976, p. 29), there is an underlying assumption that a unique and oppressed black American ethnicity exists. While this assumption is not widely known or accepted by scholars, we feel that sufficient evidence exists to warrant Bell's assumption. Roger Bastide, *Les Arneriques noires*, Payot, Paris, I967, seems to be the most extensive research in modern times. He concludes that black Americans do indeed have a unique linguistic and cultural heritage which, while being American, is different from that of Anglo-Americans, and approaches to varying degrees that of certain West African cultures. Hans Heinz Jalen, in his book *Mantu*, Grove Press, New York, 1962, lends support to this conclusion. However, it is obvious that many black American linguistic and cultural characteristics are much closer to that of Anglo-American than to any African culture. Thus it is not our contention to beat the drum for the Africanness of black American culture; we simply intend to suggest that it is a unique American culture resembling that of Anglo-Americans, but of African origins under unique historical circumstances, in a manner similar to the Irish and English cultures of today. The following references support the idea of a unique black American ethnicity: John W. Blassingame, *The Slave Cornmunity*, Oxford University Press, New York, 1972, pp.1-76; Georgia Writers Workshop, *Drum and Shadows*, University of Georgia Press, Atlanta, 1942; A. G. Nelson, *The Dawn Appears*, South Carolina Bicentennial Committee, Columbia, South Carolina, 1976.

53 Although we will only use examples of national minorities to illustrate the international law view, international human rights law as presently interpreted by the United Nations does not make a clear differentiation between national and immigrant minorities. It provides the same rights for both. Nevertheless, a short glance at the practice of most countries and at the minority treaties will show that traditionally minority rights were associated mostly with national minorities (see Part One, Chapter 3). However, in a partly or completely organized international system such as our present one, the United Nations and World Court may interpret legal principles on the basis of consensus, in accordance with "*Jus Acquun*" as opposed to "*Jus Strictum*".

54 Here we refer to an accepted legal principle on which it can be effectively argued that all minority rights depend, one without which even the human rights of individual members of minorities would be compromised. See Part One, Chapters 3 and 4 for details.

55 The principle would have to meet the requirements of Article 38 of the Statute of the World Court, which concerns the criterion for determining the principles and rules of international law.

56 The legal principle concerned will play a key role by defining the general principles of international law in relation to minorities that would become legal rules in the U.S. if the major human rights treaties are ratified by the U.S. Senate.

57 Basically, special measures means the granting of the necessary rights (other than the same rights as the majority) by which the equality between majority and minority will be ensured. Such rights are numerous, and may include assimilation at one

extreme, or political independence at the other extreme. In most modern cases the solution to minority problems has fallen somewhere between the two extremes.

58 This must be true in the cases where a minority has been thus defined by international law, and does not have the desire to assimilate.

59 It has been observed that the same six human rights treaties that include the chief principles of collective rights as it concerns minorities are also most often referred to by scholars when dealing with the concept of human rights in general. These are:
   1. International Covenant on Economic, Social and Cultural Rights
   2. International Covenant on Civil and Political Rights
   3. Optional Protocol to the International Covenant on Civil and Political Rights
   4. Convention on the Prevention and Punishment of the Crime of Genocide
   5. International Convention on the Elimination of All Forms of Racial Discrimination
   6. Convention on the Non-Applicability of Statutory Limitations to War Crimes and Crimes Against Humanity

   In this research, we refer to these six as the major human rights treaties. All six have been signed but not ratified by the U.S.. Article 27 is part of one such treaty, the covenant on Civil and Political Rights.

60 Credibility in its most exact sense refers to the fundamental principle of 'good faith' in international law. That is, that the state's intentions are in accordance with what it says, and with the principles of international law. See also Merle, *ibid.*.

61 The most obvious area of concern is the U.S. historical denial of important aspects of human rights to the black minority, the American Indians, the Chicanos and other national minorities in the U.S..

62 Here we refer to human rights principles such as "the right to leave and return to one's country", which chiefly concern the human rights efforts of the Jewish minority in the U.S.S.R. to leave the U.S.S.R. and emigrate to Israel.

63 Apart from the World Court, law determining agencies first includes the organs of the United Nations. See Article 38 of the Statutes of the World Court. Also see Part One, Introduction and Chapter 5.

64 For details on the nature of the inductive approach see Georg Schwarzenberger, *The Inductive Approach to International Law,* Stevens and Sons, London, 1965; also see Georg Schwarzenberger, *Making International Law Work,* Stevens and Sons, London, 1946; and Georg Schwarzenberger, *International Law as Applied by International Courts and Tribunals,* Vol. 3, Stevens and Sons, London, 1976. This approach recognizes the important role of power politics in problems of international law. See Introduction, Part One; and Wolfgang Friedmann, Oliver J. Lissitzyn, Richard C. Pugh, *International Law: Cases and Materials,* West Publishing Co., St. Paul, Minnesota, 1969.

65 During the Alliance For Progress, the U.S. initiated a policy of attempting to strengthen liberalism in Latin politics through increased economic assistance to target countries. While capitalism prevailed, political and social liberalism fail to grow roots. Notes from 1973 interview with Director of AIM, Mr. George Reagan, in Algiers, Algeria, North Africa.

66 Jan Tinbergen, *Rio—Reshaping the International Order,* a Report to the Club de Rorne, Antony J. Dolman, Editor, 1977. In this report, we are advised that the survival of mankind may depend on the establishment of an effective international legal system, etc.. Thus, problems as complex and as explosive as the problem of minorities must be dealt with by international law and the international institutions which report to promote international peace and justice.

67 The above principles are often referred to by numerous scholars of international law; however, Chapter 4 (pp. 85-107) of Georg Schwarzenberg and George Keeton's book, *The Inductive Approach to International Law, op. cit.*, provides an in-depth analysis.

68 *Ibid.*, p. 98.

69 Gould and Barkun, *op. cit.*, pp. 126-27.

70 Here the route of the political scientists need not be blocked by the realization that powerful states will tend to have their way. When the question of how the powerful states go about having their way (short of war) is raised, the obvious answer is by influencing less powerful states to accept their ideas; thus, although a law determining agency may in actuality be controlled by one or a few states, the majority opinion or decisions produced by the particular agency will most likely reflect the hidden political reality. In the introduction to this research, we discussed how the United Nations' decisions over the years have reflected changes in the power relationship between the U.S.S.R. and the U.S..

71 Schwarzenberger and Keeton, *op. cit.*, p. 21.

72 The Sub-Commission is a sub-commission of the Commission of Human Rights, which is a commission of the Economic and Social Council of the United Nations. In the 1960's special "rapporteur" M. Francesco Capotorti was called upon to initiate a study on the question of minority rights in relation to Article 27 of the Covenant on Civil and Political Rights. His report was presented to and accepted by a majority of the Sub-Commission in 1977. It appeared in the form of U.N. Doc. E/CN.4/Sub.2/384/Addenda. We will discuss the importance of this document in a later chapter.

73 Human Rights Commission of the Economic and Social Council.

74 During the March 1978 Meeting of the Commission, it was decided to transmit the Sub-Commission's report to member states for study and comment, and to publish the work of the special rapporteur, Mr. Francesco Capotorti.

75 See General Assembly Resolution E/CN.4/Sub.2/103: "Recognizing that there exist in many States distinctive population groups possessing racial, religious, linguistic or cultural characteristics different from those of the rest of the population, usually known as minorities."

76 E/CN.4/Sub.2/284/Add 2.

77 General Assembly Resolution E/CN.4/Sub.2/103, *loc. cit.*.

78 E/CN.4/Sub.2/SR.48, Official Records of the General Assembly, Third Session, Part 1, Sixth Committee, 83rd meeting.

79 U.N. Doc. E/CN.4/Sub.2/384/Add 2, page 80.

80 E/CN.4/Sub.2/384/Add. 1, p. 4. (a) (d) and (e) give the chief circumstances explored when considering whether it is correct to classify a group as a minority. (b) and (f) cite the chief characteristics of minorities that are not afforded international protection.

81 U.N. Doc. E/CN.4/Sub.2/384/Add 1. 82 U.N. Doc. E/CN.4/Sub.2/384/Add. 1, p. 29. 83 U.N. Doc. E/CN.4/Sub.2/384/Add. 2, p. 66.

82 U.N. Doc. E/CN.4/Sub.2/384/Add 1, p. 29.

83 U.N. Doc. E/CN.4/Sub.2/384/Add. 2, p. 66.

84 U.N. Doc. E/CN.4/Sub.2/384/Add. 6, p. 10. National minorities would by definition compose autochthonous populations.

85 U.N. Doc. E/CN.4/Sub.2/384/Add. 3, p. 13. This comment suggests a greater need of such minorities for international protection. Most national minorities would be of this type.

86 U.N. Doc. E/CN.4/Sub.2/384/Add. 1, p. 22.

87 In our view, such a social minority would be included under the sub-group minority denotation.

88 *Ibid.* The problem of tribes or extended families seems to arise out of the unique political needs facing underdeveloped countries; underdeveloped countries need special considerations, but the principle of minority rights is perhaps more important in such areas.

89 E/CN.4/Sub.2/384/Add. 3, p. 16. Our conclusion that this applies to the U.S. is derived from our historical analysis in Part Two.

90 E/CN.4/Sub.2/384/p. 5. For the U.S. position, see Anthony Lewis, "The Bakke Case", *N.Y. Times*, August 8, 1977. Also note that Articles 2:2 and 5 of the Convention on the Elimination of All Forms of Racial Discrimination call for the elimination of discrimination against minorities in exactly the manner the U.S. has labelled "reverse discrimination".

91 E/CN.4/Sub.3/384/Add. 3, p. 17. 92 E/CN.4/Sub.2/384/Add. 1, p. 31. 93 E/CN.4/Sub.2/384/Add. 1, p. 5. 94 E/CN.4/Sub.2/384/Add. 5, p. 97.

92 E/CN.4/Sub.2/384/Add. 1, p. 31.

93 E/CN.4/Sub.2/384/Add. 1, p. 5.

94 E/Cn.4/Sub.2/384/Add. 5, p. 97.

95 Carl Doka, Pro Helvetia Foundation, *Switzerland's Four National Languages*, Zurich, 1973.

96 See Arthur de Balogh, "La protection internationale des minorites", *Les Editions internationales*, Paris, 1930, pp. 23-25; T.H. Bagley, *General Principles and Problems in the International Protection of Minorities*, Imprimeries populaires, Genève, 1950, pp. 65-66; Jacques Fouques-Duparc, *La protection des rninorités de race, de langue et de religiion,* Librairie Daloz, Pans, 1922, pp. 75-77.

97 Original minorities on the following pages will be highlighted with an asterisk.*

98 According to Bagley, the above-mentioned article should be interpreted as referring to the cultural identity of the minorities mentioned. See Bagley, *op. cit.,* p. 66; and Tore Modeen, *The International Protection of National Minorities in Europe,* Abo, Finland, Abo Akademi, 1969, p. 47.

99 British and Foreign State Papers, 1829-1830, Vol. XVII, James Ridgway and Sons, London, 1832, p. 191.

100 British and Foreign State Papers, 1855-1856, Vol. XLVI, William Ridgway, London, 1965, pp. 8-18.

101 British and Foreign State Papers, 1877-1878, Vol. LXIX, William Ridgway, London, 1885, pp. 749-767.

102 British and Foreign State Papers, 1880-1881, Vol. LXXII, William Ridgway, London, 1885, pp. 382-387.

103 Claude L. Inis, Jr., *National Minorities, an International Problem,* Harvard University Press, Cambridge, Mass., 1955, pp. 8-9.

104 Excerpts from these instruments appear in *Protection of Minorities*, United Nations Publication, Sales No. 67, XIV, 3.

105 Although usually referred to as predominantly black newspapers, television stations, universities, etc., they are usually controlled by Jewish or Anglo-American capital and thus represent the general U.S. assimilationist culture.

106 E/CN.4/Sub-2/384/Add-4, P 95

107 E/CN.4/Sub.2/384/Add.4. p. 231.

108 E/CN.4/SUb.2/384/Add.3. p. 34 and 35.

109 E/CN.4/Sub.2/384/Add.4. p. 124.

110 E/CN.4/Sub-2/384/Add.3. P. 3.
111 E/CN.4/Sub.2/384/Add.4. p. 9.
112 E/CN.4/Sub.2/384/Add.l. p. 36.
113 E/CN.4lSub.2l384lAdd.3. P. 5.
114 E/CN.4/Sub.2/384 pp 70, 75.
115 There have been many charges that the Canadian government attempted to abandon the minority protection spirit of the British North America Act after World War 11 in favor of the U.S. assimilationist model.
116 E/CN.4/Sub.2/384/Add.4. p. 6.
117 Although some recent scholars have found supports for minority protection in the U.N. Charter, this does not alter the fact that the Charter does not specifically deal with the question of minority protection. See Louis B. Sohn, "The Human Rights Law of the Charter", *Texas International Law Journal*, Vol. 12, No. 2, 1977, pp. 129-39.
118 Official Records of the General Assembly, Third Session, Part 1, Annexes, Agenda Item 58, Document A/784.
119 U.N. Doc. E/CN.4/Sub.2/384/Add.2, p. 45. Also see Claydon, *loc. cit.*. He denotes the role played by the U.K. and U.S. in the early U.N. meetings against the traditional minority protection concept.
120 Extracts from these resolutions appear in the document entitled *Protection of Minorities*, United Nations Publications, Sales No. 67, XIV 4, pp. 40-46.
121 Some of the more important of these documents are listed below. E/CN.4/Sub.2/367, study of the legal validity of the undertakings concerning minorities; E/CN.4/Sub.2/6, the international protection of minorities under the League of Nations; E/CN.4/Sub.2/8, definition of the expressions 'prevention of discrimination" and 'protection of minorities"; E/CN.4/Sub.2/80, contribution of the Convention on the Prevention and Punishment of the Crime of Genocide, to the Prevention of Discrimination and the Protection of Minorities; E/CN.4/Sub.2/81, 83, 84, 85, activities of organs of the United Nations in the field of prevention of discrimination and protection of minorities; E/CN.4/Sub.2/85, definition and classification OI minorities, United Nations Publication, Sales No. 50, XIV 3;E/CN.4/Sub.2/133, treaties and international instruments concerning the protection of minorities 1919-1951; E/CN.4/Sub.2/194, activities of the United Nations relating to the protection of minorities; E/CN.4/Sub.2/L.45, Provisions for the protection of minorities, *Protection of Minorities*, United Nations Publication, Sales no. 67, XIV 4. This booklet contains the following two documents: a) compilation of the texts of those international instruments and similar measures of an international character which are of contemporary interest and which provide special protective measures for ethnic, religious or linguistic groups (E/CN.4/Sub.2/214) and b) special protective measures of an international character for ethnic, religious or linguistic groups (E/CN.4/Sub.2/221); E/CN.4/Sub.2/384 and Addenda, study of the rights of persons belonging to ethnic, religious and linguistic minorities.
122 See *Serninar on the Multinational Society*, Ljubljana, Yugoslavia, 8-21 June 1965 (ST/TAO/HR/23); *Serninar on the Prornotion and Protection of the Hurnan Rights of National, Ethnic and Other Mmorities*, Ohrid, Yugoslavia, 25 June - 8 July 1974 (ST/TAO/HR/49).
123 *Hurnan Rights: a Cornpilation of International Instrurnents of the United Nations*, United Nations Publication, Sales No. E.73 XIV 2. For information concerning ratifications as of 31 December 1976, see *Multilateral Treaties in Respect of which the Secretary-General Perforrns Depositary Functions: List of Signatures,*

Ratifications, Accessions, etc., as of 31 December 1976, United Nations Publication, Sales No. E. 77 V.7.

124 This Convention entered into force on June 2, 1959. For the text, United Nations, Treaty Series, Vol. 328, p. 249, 1959.

125 By effective measures, we assume that the United Nations Commission meant putting the principles of the ILVCR into an article of a major covenant which, once signed and ratified by member states, would become a legally binding rule of law.

126 Report of the Sub-Commission on Prevention of Discrimination and Protection of Minorities, E/CN.4/Sub.2/106/Rev. 1.

127 E/CN.4/Sub.2/108 and E/CN.4/Sub.2/106/Rev. 1.

128 *Official Records of the Economic and Social Council*, Sixteenth Supplement No. 8, E/247, paras. 51-56.

129 Not only is this one of the terms of U.N. Doc. E/CN.4/Sub.2/384, but it can also be abstracted from the practices of civilized nations.

130 *Ibid.* When we refer to secondary minority rights, we refer to all the other minorities and human rights to which members of minorities are entitled once they are officially recognized and able to maintain their ethnic identity as called for in the primary and general principle represented in Article 27.

131 Joseph B. Kelly, "National Minorities in International Law", *Denver Journal of International Law and Policy,* Vol. 3, No. 2, Fall 1973.

132 National Association for the Advancement of Colored People.

133 This notion may be easily abstracted from a study of the practices of civilized nations, and of the manner in which disputes concerning the desires and status of minorities were settled by the League of Nations. "...the League's introduction of the notion of (international) jurisdictional supervision was an important innovation... The League's instruments for the protection of minorities provided for the intervention of the Permanent Court of International Justice in cases where differences of opinion arose (between the Government of the League committees concerned and any of the allied or associated powers or any other power which was a member of the Council of the League of Nations) relating to the interpretation and application of the treaty provisions concerning minorities." See U.N. Doc. E/CN.4/Sub.2/384/Add. 2, p. 32.

134 Northern Ireland Discussion Paper 3, The Government of Northern Ireland, Northern Ireland Office HMSO, 1975, pp. 3-27.

135 Draft Covenants on Economic, Social, Cultural, Civil and Political Rights. Text approved by the Commission on Human Rights at its tenth Session, February 23 - April 16, 1954, ESCOR XVIII, Supp. 7 (E/2573), pp. 62-72.

136 Subrata Roy Chowdhury, "The Status and Norms of Self-Determination in Contemporary International Law", *Texas International Law Journal*, Vol. 12, No. 129, 1977, pp. 72-85. Also see Emerson, *loc. cit.*.

137 See United Nations Charter entered into force October 24, 1945, U.S. Department of State, Facsimile of the Charter of the United Nations, (US, DS, Publ. 2368), pp. 1-2.

138 See "Right to Enjoy Culture: International Cultural Development and Co-operation", Article XI, paragraph 1, Human Rights United Nations Publication, *loc. cit.*

139 United Nations Charter, first paragraph: situation under which the United Nations can "in defacto" intervene in the domestic affairs of a state.

140 Self-determination need not always mean independence. See Eisuke Suzuke,

"Self-Determination and World Public Order," *Virginia Journal of International Law,* Vol. 16, No. 4, Summer 1976, pp. 778-862.

141 In cases like those of the Muslim minority in India, the Algerian minority, the Bangladesh minority, etc., demands for self-determination led to the emergence of new states. However, in other situations such as the Irish Catholic minority in Northern Ireland, the Ibo minority in Nigeria, etc., demands led to special status guaranteed by new constitutional law and amendments. See M.G. Kaladharan Nayar, "Self-Determination Beyond the Colonial Context", *Texas International Law Joumal,* Vol. 10, No. 2, Spring 1975, pp. 321-45.

142 Economically, we think of the imperialist-dependency structures that exist between many states, and relationships between groups within countries, etc., and the consequences of attempting to apply any notion of binding right of self-determination. Politically, we think of the nation-state centered system and particularly of the national unity problems of former colonial countries, etc.. See also Friedmann, Lissitzyn and Pugh, *Intemational Law, op.cit.,* pp. 243-48 and 642-98.

143 See the case of Switzerland, Sweden and Belgium, Part One, Chapters 2 and 3. In all these examples, we see numerous governmental divisions and departments whose chief purpose is to provide special measures for minority protection.

144 Andrew Parkins, "Ethnic Politics: A Comparative Study of Two Immigrant Societies, Australia and the United States",*The Journal of Commonwealth and Cornparative Politics,* Vol. XV, No.l, March 1977, p. 25; see also Louis Hartz, *The Founding of New Societies,* Harcourt, Brace and World, New York, 1964.

145 The U.S. view of collective rights as it pertains to national minorities shall henceforth be abbreviated: USVCR.

146 National minorities in the U.S. consist of the following: indigenous Hawaiians, the American Indians, the Chicanos, the black Americans, the Spanish, the Acadians of Louisiana, and the indigenous population of Alaska and the Virgin Islands, etc..

147 See L.M. Romero, "Legal Education of Chicano Students: a Study in Mutual Accommodation and Cultural Conflict," *New Mexico Law Review,* Vol. 5, May 1975, pp. 177-231; Wilcomb E. Washburn, "The Historical Context of American Indian Legal Problems," *Law and Contemporary Problems,* Vol. XL, No. 1, Winter 1976, pp. 12-25; Haywood Burns, "Black People and the Tyranny of American Law," *American Academy of Political and Social Science Annals,* Vol. 407, May 1973, pp. 156-166; George Jackson, *Blood in my Eye,* Random House, New York, 1972; *United States v. James,* 528 F 2d 999 U.S. Court of Appeals 5th Cir., March 19, 1976, in Judicial Decisions, *American Journal of International Law,* Vol. 70, No. 4, October 1976, p. 835; Editorial, "Le problème des minorités," L*es dossiers de l'histoire,* no. 9, septembre-octobre 1977, pp. 70-73.

148 The recent pro and con discussion on the Bakke case bears out the existence of this concept and the type of problems involved in its implementation. See the following newspaper articles: Damon Stetson, "Affirmative-Action Order by Carey Exceeded Authority, Court Says," *N.Y. Times,* September 2, 1977; Paul Delaney, "Government to Back Minorities Admissions - Bell will File High Court Brief on College Quota Issue," *N.Y. Times,* August 23, 1977; Anthony Lewis, "The Bakke Brief," *N.Y. Times,* September 8, 1977; Washington, "Justice Agency Holds Civil Rights Act Does Not Apply to the Bakke Case," N.Y. Times, November 1, 1977.

149 According to Richard Hofstadter, the U.S. Constitution and institutions are regarded as sacred to the American people. All problems are thought to be soluble without any radical or noticeable changes in the Constitution, and the political units which it recognizes. No constitutional law (though amended) can be deleted as out of date, etc; the U.S. Constitution is eternal. See Richard Hofstadter, *The American Political Tradition and the Men Who Made It*, Vintage Books, New York, 1948.

150 Derrick A. Bell, "Racial Remediation: a Historical Perspective on Cur-rent Conditions, " *Notre Dame Lawyer*, Vol. 52, No.5, p. 5.

I5l No. 76-811, *Regents of the University of Califomia, Petitioner v. Allan Bakke*, June 28, 1978. The syllabus of this case was presented in *The United States Law Week*, 46 LW 4896, June 27, 1978, p. 37.

152 See Chicago AP, "Busing Tensions Flare in Chicago, Louisville," *The Comell Daily Sun*, July 9, 1977; Washington (UPS), "Carter to Use School Aid Funds to Step Up Race of Integration," *N.Y. Times*, August 25, 1977, p. 36.

153 See "500 Homosexuals March to the United Nations in a Rights Protest," *N.Y. Times*, August 21, 1977.

154 U.S. Senator Ervin (110 Congressional Records at 5612) found occasion to express a similar observation when speaking of Title VI of the 1964 Civil Rights Act. He stated: "The word 'discrimination' as used in this reference has no contextual explanation whatever, other than the provision that the discrimination 'is to be against' individuals participating in or benefiting from federally assisted programs and activities on the ground specified. With this context, the discrimination condemned by this reference occurs only when an individual is treated unequally or unfairly because of his race, color, religion, or national origin. What constitutes unequal or unfair treatment? Section 601 and section 602 of title VI do not say. They leave the determination of that question to the executive department or agencies administering each program, without any guideline whatever to point out what is the congressional intent."

155 International law recommends assimilation only in the case of immigrant minorities and tolerates assimilation between ethnies that have been given and properly informed of all other alternatives; which, having this information and being aware of alternatives, freely choose (by majority voice) a politics of assimilation. Forced assimilation is forbidden in international human rights law. See the following previously cited works: J. Claydon, "The Transnational Protection of Ethnic Minorities: a Tentative Framework for Enquiry," *The Canadian Yearbook of International Law*, Vol. XIII, 1975; J.B. Kelly, "National Minorities as Legal Persons in International Law," *Denver Journal of Intemational Law and Policy*, Vol. 3, No. 2, 1973, pp. 253-75.

156 Michael Novak, *The Rise of the Unrneltable Ethnics*, MacMillan Company, New York 1972.

157 Colin Greer, *Divided Society, the Ethnic Experience in America*, Basic Books, New York, 1974.

158 See Walter L. Fleming, *Documentary History of Reconstruction*, Arthur H. Clark Company, Cleveland, 1906 (Vol. 1, Section 9, Chapter 11, "Opinions of C.P. Huntington," pp. 155-56 and Vol.2, Sections 1-5, Chapter XIII, "The Undoing of Reconstruction," pp. 381-423).

159 Bell, *op. cit.*, p. 6. Professor Bell expresses this same notion but only as it relates to the black minority. *Le Monde*, "Porto-Rico en quête d'identité," 05-10-77, p. 1,

Alain-Marie Carron writes: "Le travail que la race anglaise a commencé lorsqu'elle a colonisé l'Amérique du nord est destiné à se poursuivre jusqu'à ce que tout territoire sur la terre qui n'est pas déjà le siège d'une vieille civilisation soit devenue anglais".

160 In this book, dominance is used in the sense of its use in dependency theory. It may or may not imply intentions or will, but it always implies economic and socio-political control or asymmetry in relationships between the smaller and larger entities.

161 This expression seems to provide support for the notion suggested in *The Question of Imperialism* by Benjamin Cohen, that a state can practice domestic imperialistic policies of domination, inequality (political and economic), and exploitation where a stronger majority ethny (or nation) and a weaker minority ethny (or nation) live within the political boundaries of the same state. Cohen writes: "The point is simply that an action which involves the political domination or control of one country over another, or of one national group within a country over another, must be labelled imperialistic. If the term imperialism is limited to maritime empires, analysis runs the risk of being incomplete. Colonies overseas are but one special case of a much more general social phenomenon; political dependencies at home or beyond the borders (of which there seem to be numerous examples) are of equal importance. The problem is national oppression or subjugation; the subordination of one nation by another. No specific type can be ignored." Benjamin Cohen, *The Question of Imperialism*, Basic Books, New York, 1973, p. 92. The following writings also call attention to various exploitative aspects of U.S. "domination" over its national minorities: Albert Memmi, *L'homme dominé, le noir, le colonisé, le prolétaire, le juif, la femme, le domestique*, Petite Bibliotheque Payot, Paris, 1973; John Howard, *Awakening Minorities, American Indians, Mexican Americans, Puerto Riccns*, etc., Transaction Books, New Jersey, 1972.

162 For some political scientists, the black minority in the U.S. is seen as extremely important to the future of the U.S.. See Amaury de Riencourt, *The American Empire*, Dell Publishing, New York, 1968.

163 J.O. Brown, D.J. Givelber and S.N. Subrin, "Treating Blacks as if They Were White," *The University of Pennsylvania Law Review*, Vol. 124, No. 1, November 1975, pp. 1-45. Even scholars such as Derrick Bell and many other American scholars seem unable to frame their minority problem observations in terms above the parochial national level, and thus are unable to focus the problems in such a way as to permit the experiences of other nations to play a useful role in the analysis.

164 International law in both covenants emphasizes cultural rights, includ-ing the right of self-determination. The Genocide Convention underlines the right of racial, ethnic, religious, etc. groups to exist. Cultural rights have recently been re-emphasized in the United Nations Declaration of the Principles of International Cultural Co-operation (UNESCO, November 4, 1966), etc..

165 See Novak, *loc. cit.;* Barrow, Alaska (AP), "Race Tension Rises in Alaska Town," *N.Y. Times*, 08-09-77; Reginald Stuart, "Impending Desegregation Brings Some Uneasiness to Ohio Cities," *N.Y. Times*, 28-08-77. The Alaska article speaks of the native peoples *vis-à-vis* the Anglo-American ethny of Alaska, while the Stuart article equates any community desire for territoriality as an expression of 'segregation', (here the word 'segregation' has the connotation of apartheid). Thus, any government, etc., efforts to forcibly assimilate ethnic communities,

schools, etc. becomes desegregation, and any efforts of the minority to have its historical circumstances included in the evaluation of what it needs to be equal, is considered reverse racism, should the interest of a single majority member be compromised. (See "Reverse Racism," *Newsweek Magazine,* September 14, 1977). Note how this American definition of 'reverse racism' apparently ignores the notion of eliminating discrimination against minorities as called for in Article 5, paragraph 2 of the International Covenant on the Elimination of All Forms of Racial Discrimination, 1966.

166 This type of confusion is easy to make since the words ethny and race are often used to mean the same. For example, in the October 5, 1977 issue of *Le Monde,* in an article entitled "Porto-Rico en quête d'identité," Alain-Marie Carron (see footnote 158) sees the Anglo-Saxon as a race.

167 This type of orientation can be seen clearly in *Multi-National Development in South Africa,* published by the South African State Department of Information in 1974. The author spends almost all of the book speaking about the division among the black populations as a basis for multi-national development. Only once does he proclaim the non-existence of divisions among the white population.

168 Gerard Chaliand, *Revolution in the Third World, Myth and Prospects,* Viking Press, New York, 1977, p. XI.

169 Andre Gunder Frank, "The Development of Underdevelopment," in Charles K. Wilber, *The Political Economy of Development and Underdevelopment,* Part 2, Random House, New York, 1973, pp. 94-105.

170 W.E.B. DuBois, *The World and Africa,* International Publishers, New York, 1965, pp. 64-5.

171 In his book *Muntu,* Seuil, Paris, 1961, Jahn Janheinz points out the general geographic location from which slaves were taken and the general locations to which they were brought in America. W.E.B. Dubois, in *The Suppression of the African Slave Trade to the U.S., 1638-870,* The Social Science Press, New York, 1954, provides us with the appropriate numbers.

172 Basil Davidson, *The African Slave Trade, Pre-Colonial History: 1450-1850,* Little, Brown, Boston, 1961; Wish Harvey, *Slavery in the South,* Farrar, Straus and Co., New York, 1964, a collection of contemporary accounts of the system of plantation slavery in the southern United States in the eighteenth and nineteenth centuries; and Wish Harvey,"American Slave Insurrections before 1861," *The Journal of Negro History,* Vol. XXII, No. 3, Washington, D.C., July 1937, pp. 199-321.

173 John W. Blassingame, *The Slave Cornmunity,* Oxford University Press, New York, 1972, Chapter 4, pp. 104-131. See also "The Confession of Nat Tumer" in Wish, *Slavery in the South, op.cit.,* pp.1-25 and Wish, "American Slave Insurrections before 1861," *op. cit.,* pp. 199-321.

174 Wish, *Slavery in the South, op.cit.,* p. 17. After questioning Nat Turner, Thomas R. Gray writes: "When I questioned him as to the insurrection in North Carolina happening about the same time, he denied any knowledge of it and when I looked him in the face..., he replied: 'I see Sir you doubt my word, but can you not think the same ideas, and strange appearances about this time in the heavens might prompt others... to this undertaking... ' I shall not attempt to describe the effects of his narrative, as told and commented on by himself, in a condemned hole of the prison. The calm, deliberate composure with which he spoke of his late deed and intentions, the expression of his fiend-like face when excited by

enthusiasm, still bearing the stains of blood... clothed with rags and covered with chains, yet daring to raise his manacled hands to heaven, with a spirit soaring above the attributes of man; I looked on him and my blood curdled in my veins..."

175 While we have no intentions of entering into a socio-psychological study or to proclaim an pretention to this effect, it is of use to suggest that the interaction between ethny in a slave system may have produced an illogical fear that if an ex-slave minority is given certain types of rights, it will take revenge on the ex-slave master. Derrick Bell hints of this effect when he speaks of the Anglo-American fear of inundation. See also the chapter entitled "Danger of Negro Suffrage," Blassingame, *loc. cit.* and Walter Fleming, *Documentary History of Reconstruction,* Arthur H. Clark Co., Cleveland, Ohio, 1906, pp. 117-271.

176 Herbert Aptheker, *A Documentary History of the Negro People in the U.S.,* The Citzel Press, New York, 1951, pp. 4-490. This author reports cases of revolts and runaways up until the Civil War.

177 It was not until July 21, 1868 that black Americans were officially recognized as citizens of the U.S.. See XIV Amendments, U.S. Constitution.

178 Jerome J. Shestack and Roberta Cohen, 'International Human Rights: a Role for the United States", *Virginia Journal of International Law,* Vol. 14, No. 4, Summer 1974, pp. 673-701 (quotation p. 680).

179 Indeed, this is very much the question posed by the decision in the Bakke Case. Affirmative action advocates claim that the equality of the black minority will depend on making up for past injuries; however, unless past injuries are recognized there is obviously nothing to make up for; likewise, unless the existence of the minority is recognized, there is no one to make up to, etc..

180 The possibility that this relationship created significant psychological problems can be seen in the words of such famous Americans as Alexander Hamilton. He once wrote: "The contempt we have been taught to entertain for the blacks makes us fancy many things that are founded neither in reason nor in experience." See Herbert G. Gutman, *The Black Family in Slavery and Freedom- 1750-1925,* Vintage Books, New York, 1977, p. 1.

181 *Regent of the University of California, Petitioner v. Allan Bakke, loc. cit.*

182 Wallerstein, *The Formation of the World System, loc. cit..* (Wallerstein's general analysis of the rise of capitalism would lead to the above conclusion.) See also George A. Davis and O. Fred Donalson, *Blacks in the United States: a Geographic Perspective,* Houghton Mifflin Co., Boston, 1975, pp. 53-59.

183 It was the Dred Scott Supreme Court Decision of 1866 that led to official citizenship for this minority (see Aptheker, *op. cit.,* p. 260). However, the realization of this change in status could not be manifested until years after the Civil War.

184 Leslie H. Fishel and Benjamin Quarles, *The Black American,* Scott, Foreman, Glenview, Illinois, 1970. This belief of the abolitionists will be seen again in the discussion on F. Douglass in this chapter, who was spoken of as being proof of the ability of blacks to adopt Anglo-American culture. Most abolitionists never considered any other future possible. Also, since abolitionists were also classical liberals, it is interesting to note that their ideas never interfered with a central U.S. liberal notion of the economic need for cheap labor.

185 The Black Codes refer to the 1865-1866 legislation which served to regulate the status and conduct of newly freed black Americans. Also see Albert Blaustein, *Civil Rights and the American Negro,* Washington Square Press, New York, 1968, pp. 217225.

186 DuBois, *Black Reconstruction in America, op. cit.,* pp. 630-33, 694-95 and 705. Also see Leon F. Litwack, *North of Slavery, the Negro in the Free States 1790-1860,* University of Chicago Press, Chicago, 1961.

187 Wish, *Slavery in the South, op. cit.,* pp. 59-85. See also Dubois, *Black Reconstruction in America, op. cit.,* pp. 325-330, and Fleming, *op. cit.,* pp. 137-44.

188 Fleming, *op. cit.,* Vol. 2, pp. 316-397. This notion is derived from the knowledge that during the slave period the black American's humanity was not recognized by Anglo-Americans. The only humanity (culture, manners, etc.) that would have thus appeared acceptable to the slave was that of Anglo-Americans.

189 John R. Commons, *Races and Immigrants in America,* The MacMillan Company, New York, 1924, pp. 53-100, provides us with the following statistics: "In reality the Negro element during the one hundred and ten years of census taking has steadily declined in proportion to the white element. Although Negroes in absolute numbers have increased from 757,000 in 1790 to 4,442,000 in 1860, and 8,834,000 in 1900, yet in 1790 they were one fifth of the total population; in 1860 they were one seventh, and in 1900 only one ninth... in the southern states the Negro is most clearly falling behind; immigration is not a significant factor. From 1880 to 1900 the whites in eighteen southern states without the aid of foreign immigration increased 58% and the Negroes only 33%... In only two of these states, South Carolina and Mississippi, does the Negro element predominate, and in another state, Louisiana, a majority were Negroes in 1890, but a majority were whites by 1900. At the beginning of the nineteenth century, the Southern Negroes were increasing much faster than the southern whites. At the end of it, they were increasing only about three fifths as fast." Commons further informs us that during the decades of 1900-1924 (not after slavery and the Civil War period, but after the breakdown of the Reconstruction period), black Americans, by migration from the South, increased relatively faster in northern cities. The white population of Chicago increased threefold from 1880 to 1900, while the black American population increased fivefold. In Philadelphia the increase was 100% to 50% in favor of the black American population, and in thirty-eight of the largest U.S. cities, the black American population, over a period of ten years, 1914-1924, increased 38% to 33% over the Anglo-American population, including foreign immigration. The fact that a majority population of black Americans would have posed a problem for the U.S. government can be seen in the federal government's reaction to areas where they did come to political power as a majority population, which will be documented later in this chapter.

190 W.E.B. DuBois, *The World and Africa,* International Publishers, New York, 1965.

191 Harry Magdoff, *L'âge de l'imperialisrne,* Masperro, Paris, 1970.

192 Dr. Rayford and Phillip Sterling, *Four Who Took Freedom,* Doubleday and Company, Garden City, New Jersey, 1967, p. 65.

193 Sherman's field orders preceded the creation of the Freedmen's Bureau. They were issued after his victories in Georgia and South Carolina. W.E.B. DuBois reports that 10,000 black soldiers had fought with Sherman in Georgia and South Carolina.

194 This journal can be found at the South Carolina Archives in Columbia, South Carolina.

195 DuBois, *Black Reconstruction in America, op. cit.,* pp. 3-83. In these sections, DuBois emphasizes the importance of cheap labor to the U.S. economic

processes, and the willingness of the U.S. to free the slaves and make concessions to them in order to obtain that labor and/or avoid losing the war. He also implies that such concessions prevented larger black armed revolts.

196 Not only were the Anglo-Americans bitterly divided after the war, but also support elements in Europe (the seat of the major world powers) were divided as to whom they should support in the U.S. Civil War in order to obtain certain foreign policy objectives.

197 See October 16th, 1854 speech of President A. Lincoln. Paul M. Angle, Abraham Lincoln's Speeches and Letters, 1832-1865, J.M. Dent and Sons Limited, London, 1957, p. 54.

198 The syllabus of the Bakke Case, op. cit., p. 35, states: "Although the Freedmen's Bureau legislation provided aid for refugees, thereby including white persons... the bill was regarded to the dismay of many congressmen as solely and entirely for the Freedmen and to the exclusion of all other persons. Indeed the bill was bitterly opposed on the grounds of 'reverse racism' that it undertakes to make the Negro in some respects superior... and give them favors that certain poor white boys in the north cannot get.

199 Indications that elements of the U.S. government may have been tinkering with the idea of providing the black American minority with a degree of political autonomy can be seen in the 1854 speech by President Lincoln (see footnote 196, p. 54) and the actions of the occupying northern army in the south. See Fleming, op. cit., Vol. 1, pp. 73, 350-61. However, more telling evidence is the support (financial) accorded to the project. See Robert Goldston, The Negro Revolution, The New American Library, Inc., New York, 1969, p. 106. Goldston suggested that Lincoln reasoned that abolition would find more acceptance both north and south if there was a place black Americans could go to live without having to be mixed with Anglo-Americans. It was for this reason, according to Goldston, that Lincoln encouraged the congressional appropriation of large sums of money to be used by him as he saw fit to further black American colonization. At Lincoln's request, Liberia, which had been set up as a sovereign nation by the American Colonization Society in 1847, declared itself willing to receive any number of black American settlers. Other locations were also considered. (Due to the unfavorable international and national environment, Lincoln's idea, like the Freedmen's bureau, was destined to be unacceptable to many congressmen, many representing the northern business interest, who saw in the Freedmen his natural reservoir of cheap labor. Also how could the leading European powers of the period have accepted the idea of the U.S. extending the size of its colonial possessions in Africa or the Caribbean?) For details on all the U.S. colonization schemes, see Winthrop D. Jordan, White and Black: American Attitudes Towards the Negro, 1550-1812, University of North Carolina Press, 1968, pp. 517-5~0.

200 Louis Ruchames, Racial Thought in America, The University of Massachussetts Press, Boston, 1969, Vol. 1, pp. 380-1.

201 These international pressures at this time probably were concerned with uniting the colonies before the major European powers had the opportunity to use American disunity as a means of re-establishing their dominance on the North American continent. In this connection, one should remember that the U.S. had recently ended a violent dispute with England, 1776 and 1814, which was still entrenched on the continent in Canada; further, both Spain and France also had interest in America. It is not surprising that one of the first major foreign policies of the emerging United States would be the well-known Monroe Doctrine.

202 Most of this constitution's laws dealt with the question of human rights. Among its progressive measures were the following: abolition of discrimination against race and color, particularly in the militia and public schools; granting of suffrage to all males; making education available to both ethnic groups; abolition of property qualifications for voting or holding office; the increase of women's rights so that the property of married women could not be sold for their husband's debts; the provision that judges be elected rather than appointed, etc..

203 In one such instance, representative Robert Small from South Carolina campaigned for the re-election of Governor Chamberlain who lost to his opponent, governor Hampton; Ben Tillman, an Anglo-American U.S. Congressional representative from the region, bragged that it had been accomplished through stuffing ballot boxes and shooting black Americans. See Ford and Sterling, *loc. cit.*.

204 As early as 1869, federal troops had been employed into a South divided into military districts along state lines. By the time of President Hayes' decision, Congress had replaced General Saxton, federal administrator in this region, and federal troops had compelled landholding black Americans to leave their land and to make contracts, often with their former owners, as laborers. See DuBois, *Black Reconstruction in America, op. cit.*, pp. 381-430.

205 Howard K. Beale, *Theodore Roosevelt and the Rise of America to World Power,* Collier MacMillan Limited, London, 1967, Third Printing, p. 77.

206 Dr. W. Rayford Logan, *The Betrayal of the Negro: From Rutherford B. Hayes to Woodrow Wilson,* Collier-MacMillan Limited, London, 1969, Fourth Printing, p. 270. See also (for superior race opinions) Beale, *op. cit.*, pp. 41-46, 53, 78-80, 149-50, 2223-5, 289, 304-5.

207 See Bakke Case, *op. cit.*, p. 33.

208 Jim Crow was the period in which Anglo-Americans, particularly in the south, instituted a common colonial policy against the black Americans. Absorbed with industrial growth, cycles of economic prosperity and depression, etc., the Anglo-American majority used the black Americans' lack of education, wealth, etc. as confirmation of their biological inferiority, and justified on that basis, all forms of imperialistic exploitation. State after state changed their constitutions and instituted statutory measures designed to separate the black Americans into a totally dependent nation. For details see Blaustein and Zangrando, *op. cit.*, pp. 283-313. U.S. Supreme Court Justice Marshall also details the concept of Jim Crow: "In the wake of *Plessy*, many states expanded their Jim Crow laws. The segregation of the races was extended to residential areas, parks, hospitals, theatres, waiting rooms and bathrooms. There were even statutes and ordinances which authorized separate phone booths for Negroes and whites, which required that textbooks used by children of one race be kept separate from those used by the other. Nor were the laws restricting the rights of Negroes limited solely to the Southern states. In many of the Northern states, the Negro was denied the right to vote, prevented from serving on juries, and excluded from theatres, restaurants, hotels and inns. Under President Wilson, the federal Government began to require segregation in Government buildings; desks of Negro employees were curtained off; separate bathrooms and separate tables in the cafeterias were provided, and even the galleries of the Congress were segregated." See Bakke Case, *loc. cit.*.

209 *Brown v. Board of Education,* 347 U.S. 483, 1954. See Derrick Bell, *Race, Racism and American Law,* Tommie Smith and John Carlos, Mexico City, 1968.

210 For more information on the American Colonization Society, see Goldston, *op. cit.*, p. 92. The author tells us that "The American Colonization Society composed of prominent 'humanitarians,' had been formed in 1817. Enlisting the aid of Congress (which appropriated $100,000 for the Society) and of President James Monroe, the Society founded the colony of Liberia in 1822, on the old Gold Coast in Africa. By 1852, less than eight thousand Negroes had gone to Liberia; and of these thirty-six hundred were slaves who could only gain their freedom by promising to emigrate, while another thousand were Africans taken from captured slave ships. A major reason why free Negroes would not emigrate was their realization that the colonization scheme was a means whereby slavery as an institution could be made secure through the deportation of the troublesome free Negro."

211 George Padmore, *Pan-Africanism or Communism*, Roy Publishers, New York, 1956, p. 93.

212 Richard Wright, *12 Million Black Voices*, Viking Press, New York, 1941.

213 This is especially true with the Garvey scheme which also foresaw the liberation of Africans from colonialism and their unity into one large state to which all persons of African descent would be connected.

214 Again we wish to note that Anglo-American interest is interpreted by its ruling class; this class being both capitalist and allied to the ruling classes of the colonialist states in Europe, of course could not have been expected to assist Garvey's scheme in any way.

215 All studies which researched B.T. Washington, whether negative or positive, present him not as a man representing the popular aspirations of the black masses, but as a man bowing to the pressures of the majority ethnic group and attempting to manipulate the majority towards improved material conditions for the black minority. See L. Bennett, *Before the Marflower*, Penguin Books, Baltimore, 1966; Wright, *loc. cit.*; Gutman, *loc. cit.*; Padmore, *loc. cit.*; Dr. E. U. Essien Udom, *Black Nationalism,* The University of Chicago Press, Chicago, 1962.

216 Padmore, *op. cit.*, p. 106. DuBois overlooked adding that continually bowing to the will of the majority establishes institutions that condition the situation of oppression both nationally and internationally, including the political and legal rights and capacity for the majority to maintain the minority in the position it has so often accepted.

217 Their program was both assimilationist and idealist. It probably encouraged the movement of many black Americans from the south where a possibility for a solid political basis existed, into the Ghetto of the north where certain official and unofficial aspects of apartheid were absent. Because there was no official apartheid in the north, it encouraged black Americans to look towards the North for leadership and sanctuary, and thus maintained a check on the potential for meaningful black minority political unity in the south. See David and Donaldson, *op. cit.*, pp. 81-91.

218 *Ibid.* See also Harold Cruse, *The Crisis of the Negro Intellectual,* William Morrow and Company, Inc., New York, 1967.

219 It probably occurred this way because religious rights had gained a strong foothold in the U.S. constitution and in U.S. society in general. The history of the Mormon Church is an interesting testimony to this fact. See Allan Nevins and Henry Steel Commanger, *The Pocket History of the United States,* Pocket Books, New York, 1951, pp. 215-16. Also Islam had a sporadic survival among the slaves and ex-slaves after the Civil War. This new nationalist movement drew on the

knowledge of this survival, and on the existence of Islam in West Africa, to justify its false claims that all black Americans were, or should be, Muslim.

220 The first time black American nationalism under the guise of Islam surfaced on the American scene, it did so under the leadership of a black American called Noble Drew Ali (1886-1928), born in North Carolina, who founded the Moorish American Science Temple in Chicago. See Udom, *loc. cit.*.

221 At his home in Algiers, Algeria in 1973, the great Muslim sage Malik Benabi stated: "All streams of the oppressed of the world will flow into the ocean of Islam and the Islam of the modern world, like that of the ancient, shall become the needs and ingredients of its stream."

222 The disappearance is reported in all major works on this movement, and although there has been speculation by various news journals, such as the *New York Times,* September 1977, as to his fate, there seems to be little conclusive evidence of what really happened to W.D. Fard. Also see Charles E. Lincoln, *The Black Muslims in the United States,* Beacon Press, Boston, 1960.

223 Here it should be mentioned that since the death of Elijah Muhammad in 1975, and his replacement by his son Warid Muhammad, the philosophy of the movement has become anti-racist and anti-nationalist, and has undergone numerous other radical reforms. See *Bilalian News,* September 1977-1978, printed by Mosque E. Muhammad, Chicago.

224 Similar to the recent position of the boxer Muhammad Ali, Elijah Muhammad had taught his followers to resist fighting in American wars until such time as they permit the black minority to acquire political control of a few states.

225 There were disturbances against the U.S. embassy in Turkey when Malcolm X was killed; Muhammad Ali was well as Louis Farrakhan and Warid Muhammad have been well received in Islamic countries; Libya has twice lent millions for Islamic development in the U.S.; Syria has invited Farrakhan to assist in negotiating the release of a captured American pilot, etc.

226 United Nations Publication, *Human Rights: A Compilation of International Instruments of the United Nations,* Sales No. E73 XIV7 (ST/LEG/SER.0/6) ST/HER/2 1977, p. 41.

227 It is usually accepted that the enforcement of anti-apartheid laws began when Presidents Eisenhower and Kennedy sent troops to enforce a higher education court decision in Arkansas and Alabama (1960 and 1963).

228 The Declaration was subsequently adopted in 1960. General Assembly Resolution 1514 (XV) of 14 December 1960.

229 *Brown v. Board of Education,* 347 U.S. 483, *loc. cit.*.

230 This was a device to prevent black Americans from voting in the southern states. They were required to pay a tax in order to be eligible.

231 Roy C. Macridis, *The Study of Comparative Government,* Random House, New York, 1955, (section on U.S.A.).

232 The U.S. system was designed to function by pressure groups, etc. working through either of the three divisions of government: the court, the legislature or the executive. By going directly to the street and mobilizing groups to disobey the law, Martin Luther King Jr. brought about a temporary dysfunction of the political system, which was evidently temporarily unable to process the demands made by the black minority.

233 Although the first publicized sit-in occurred in 1960, sit-ins in the same city were witnessed as early as 1956. These early sit-ins received no publicity and little reaction from the establishments entered. On most occasions witnessed, the sit-

in protesters were simply ignored, though on certain occasions they were served. By 1960, there were several Anglo-American restaurants in Greensboro that had begun to serve black Americans without any fanfare. Many of the students participating in the publicized sit-ins of the '60's expected to eventually be served without making a national issue.

234 Barbara Ritchie, *The Riot Report,* Viking Press, New York, 1969.

235 For further information on these groups which came to national attention during the period 1960-75, see Philip S. Foner, *The Black Panther Speaks,* Lippincott, Philadelphia, 1970- Stokely Carmichael and Hamilton Charles, *Black Power,* Random House, New York, 1967; William L. Patterson, *We Charge Genocide,* International Press, New York, 1970; and Jerome Zukrosky, "Growing Up on Integration," *The New Republic,* Vol. 167, October 14, 1972, pp. 19-22.

236 Riots occurred in Birmingham, Alabama; Savannah, Georgia; Cambridge, Maryland; Chicago; Philadelphia; Cleveland, Ohio; Brooklyn; Jersey City; Elizabeth City; and Paterson, New York, etc.. See Barbara Ritchie, *The Riot Report,* Viking Press, New York, 1969.

237 Big business and labor were not ranged in economic battle against one another over this bill; in fact, large business interests offered no visible aid and comfort to their small business brethren. With or without the 1964 Civil Rights Act, black American labor would still be available to meet big business's cheap labor needs. This conclusion is derived from a study of forces opposing the end of apartheid in the United States. Large business interests were spectacular in their absence. A case in point can be seen in the lack of support afforded Governor Wallace in his Alabama stand against restaurant integration. The Anglo-American artisan and shopkeeper were left to their own devices.

238 Ritchie, *op. cit.,* pp. 25-33. There were 150 riots in 150 different cities during the summer of 1965 alone.

239 To this writer, working as an employee at the New York City Social Services Department at the time of Martin Luther King's death and during the first series of riots to follow, it seemed as if the entire U.S. was focused on the outcome of each encounter. The main news reports in Time Square were concerned primarily with riot reports; Time Square itself had all but ceased to function. Peoples of various ethnicities stood around in small groups, eyes focused on the flashing news bulletins. A factor not often observed by scholars on this subject is that at the height of such disorders in Harlem or Washington, D.C., Arabs, Chinese and Puerto Ricans (some as white or blond as Anglo-Americans) walked unhesitatingly through these areas carrying on their business as best they could. It seemed that the rioters' anger was focused primarily against any symbols of the U.S. system, including the chief perpetrators of that system: Anglo-Americans.

240 This may have been accomplished using Article 11:2 of the United Nations Charter.

241 The New Republic of Africa, the Garveyists, the Black Nationalists, etc..

242 NAACP, Urban League, Southern Christian Leadership Conference (Martin Luther King's group), etc..

243 The Black Panthers, the U.S. Communist Party, Malcolm X's O.A.A.U..

244 This is due to well-known American traditions of southerners being opposed to civil rights or human rights as they relate to the national minorities in the U.S..

245 B. Pitman, *Doctrines arnéricaines de droit international,* bulletin., No. 1-2, Publications de la Conciliation Internationale, Pans, 1937; William A. Williams, *The Tragedy of American Diplomacy,* Dell Publishing Co., Inc, New York, 1972.

246 The Civil Rights Act of l964 was addressed essentially to middle class needs. There was no demand to alter the economic status quo. With or without the 1964 Civil Rights Act, black American labor would still be available to meet business needs for cheap labor.

247 While the chief obstacle to civil rights legislation in the past had come from the Senate, in 1964 Senate minority leader Everett M. Dirksen, a Republican, led many cf his Republican troops out of the Conservative coalition to join with northern democrats to beat back the southern Democratic challenge. In the House of Representatives, Democrat Emmanuel Celler, whose House Judiciary Committee had control of the 1964 bill, collaborated closely with his Republican colleague, William M. McCulloch, to forge a similar relationship. Consulting closely with Justice Department officials, these two men and their committee wrote an extremely strong bill which remained largely intact as it wound its way first through the House and then through the Senate. See Macridis, *loc. cit.*. Also see Richard Bardolph, *The Civil Rights Record: Black American and the Law 1849-1970*, Crowell Publication Company, New York, 1970.

248 The struggle against the passage of the 1964 Civil Rights Act was led by Senators James Eastland of Mississippi and Richard Russell of Georgia, both of whom were based in states which in 1960 had either predominantly black (Mississippi) or evenly-divided racial populations. To thwart Eastland's power in committee, the Senate leadership decided on a tactic to delay developing a Senate bill and instead to accept a previously passed House version. While Senate rules required that legislation initiated in the Senate first be routed through the standing committees, House-sponsored legislation, upon reception from the lower house, could be placed immediately on the calendar for consideration on the floor. Because it thus could not be killed in committee, the Civil Rights Bill of 1964 brought forth a southern filibuster, or "extended debate" on the Senate floor, led by Senator Russell. On June 8, 1964, more than three months after having first received the House Bill, the Senate at last ended the southern filibuster by invoking cloture, by a vote of 71-29. A few days later, the legislation was voted into law. See Bardolph, *op. cit.,* p. 425. Also see William Keefe and Morris S. Oqui, *The American Legiislative Process*, 4th edition, Prentice-Hall, Englewood Cliffs, New Jersey, 1977.

249 Derrick A. Bell, Race, *Racism and American Law*, Tommie Smith and John Carlos, Mexico, 1969, pp. 14-15. The following were among the instances Bell cited to substantiate this opinion:

(a) The summary expulsion of several black college students for participation in a 1960 sit-in protest led to the landmark fifth circuit decision in *Dixon v. Alabama State College*, which recognized the entitlement of college students to specific due process protections when faced with serious disciplinary action. Those guarantees, later extended by the Supreme Court to public school students, unfortunately have provided little help to the thousands of black American children suspended or expelled in the school desegregation process.

(b) The Court challenge to Virginia's blatant effort to stifle desegregation litigation by altering the state's canons of professional conduct to bar procedures used by civil rights lawyers resulted in *NAACP v. Button*. There, the Supreme Court recognized civil rights litigation as a form of political association and expression protected by the Constitution. This important victory simply left civil rights forces where they were, able but still required to fight segregation through the courts. In a few years, however, unions and other associations had utilized *NAACP v.*

Button to upset state bar restrictions against group legal practices with potential, although still little, realized benefits for millions of middle-class Americans. The more recent case of *Allan Bakke v. University of California* was not mentioned by Bell. However, this case involved the use of Title VI of the 1964 civil rights act originally enacted (under the guise of extending civil rights to the black minority) to prevent minority preferential treatment and maintain Anglo-American domination over all professional and economic areas, etc. of U.S. life. U.S. Supreme Court Justice Blackman's approach suggested the inevitability of this development. He stated: 'The theoretical solution to this problem (special measures for minorities in education) would be to enlarge our graduate schools. Then all who desired and were qualified could enter and talk of discrimination would vanish. Unfortunately, this is neither feasible nor realistic. The vast resources that apparently would be required simply are not available."

250 The first was the Freedman Bureau which was set up after the Civil War to help bring order, etc., to black Americans, ex-Union troops and refugees. See Chapter 2. Notably, both followed periods of social, economic and political disorder marked by protest within the black American community.

251 Johnson stated: "Let your search be free... as best you can find the truth and express it in your report... this matter is far too important for politics." See Foreword, *The Riot Report.* From the orientation of the report, one might assume Johnson was only concerned with domestic bipartisan politics not influencing the report. It is unlikely, for international reasons, he wanted the report to show a conflict caused by majority-minority inequality.

252 In fact the Report's conclusion would seem to belie such a historical pattern altogether, when it made the following assertion: "Our nation is moving toward two societies, one black, one white, separate and unequal." See Ritchie, *op. cit.*, p. 1. Further clarification of the term 'relational inequality' as it concerns the U.S. national minorities can be seen in Michael J. Perry's article, 'The Disproportionate Impact Theory of Racial Discrimination," *University of Pennsylvania Law Review,* Vol. 125:540, 1977, pp. 539-88. In this article, he speaks about the emergence of the disproportionate racial impact theories which in general demonstrate that equal access civil rights legislation, in general, does not provide the national minorities with the same societal potential as obtained by the Anglo-American majority. Also, this concept is often seen in connection with imperialism and dependence studies. In these studies, it is called 'relational inequality' and refers to the imperialistic or dependency relationship existing between nations or ethnicities. Cohen, *loc. cit..* During a debate at the United Nations between members of the Group of 77 and a spokesman for the advanced western nations, a Pakistani representative summed this idea up in the following words: "Equal rights among unequals is not equitable."

253 The following articles evidence the persisting and increasing problems facing the black American minority since the end of the riots period. See Editorial, "Racial Disorders: Remember the Kemer Commission Report," *N.Y. Times,* October 19, 1977;(UPI) "Unemployed Black Youth Reach Record Numbers as Whites Make Gains," *N.Y. Times,* August 21, 1977; James Wooten, "Carter Delay on Endorsing Bill Linked to 4% Unemployment Provision," *N.Y. Times,* October 20, 1977, p. A-12; Robert Wilkins, 'The Bakke Case: Old Allies Split: Many Blacks Distressed by End of Consensus," *N.Y. Times,* October 20, 1977, p. A-12; Augustin Togang, "Aux USA la presse noire lutte pour sa part du marché," *Le Devoir,* June 25, 1977;

Art L. Goldman, 'Teachers Union Refuses to Back Minority Quotas," *N.Y. Times*, August 10, 1977; Damond Stetson, "Affirmative Action Order by Carey Exceeded Authority, Court Says," *N.Y. Times*, 02-09-77; G. Bolton, "Trend in Black Homicides is Shock to Researcher," *N.Y. Times*, 08-09-77; C. Hunter Gault, "Key Blacks Planning Attack on Neglect Meeting to Coordinate Strategies for Drive: Is First Since 1960," *N.Y. Times*, August 19, 1977; (UPI) Washington, "Carter Urged to Oppose Race Quotas at Colleges," *N.Y. Times*, 08-09-77 .

254 Editorial, "Racial Disorders: Remember the Kemer Commission Report," *N.Y. Times*, October 19, 1977. The Editor writes: 'Ten years ago the National Advisory Commission on Civil Disorder, created by President Johnson, sought to resolve the burgeoning problem of racial disorders in American cities... To date, most of the commission's recommendations have been ignored."

255 The constants in U.S. minority-majority relations are domination of the minority by the majority and provision of only those rights that are assumed to maintain politico-economic domination in the interest of the majority ethny as interpreted by the ruling classes of that ethny.

256 Here we suggest that the basic philosophy of the U.S. government apparently remained the same as the constants mentioned above; however, the method of maintaining these constants under changed domestic and international conditions demanded a switch from a method of apartheid to one of assimilation. Americans make no difference between assimilation and integration. In the writings of several scholars even biological assimilation was spoken of along with integration. See conclusion for the international law view of these terms.

257 Bakke case. *op. cit.*, p. 34.

258 Also the lack of such a program is emphasized by the lack of standard or well-defined definitions of such key terms as discrimination, even in key civil rights acts. On page 22 of the Bakke Case syllabus, *op. cit.*, Justices Brennan, White and Blackmun issued the following statement: 'Indeed, there was a strong emphasis throughout Congress' consideration of Title VI on providing the Executive Branch with considerable flexibility in interpreting and applying the prohibition against racial discrimination. Attorney General Robert Kennedy testified that regulations had not been written into the legislation itself because the rules and regulations defining discrimination might differ from one program to another so that the term would assume different meaning in different contexts."

259 "Minorities in the earlier Islamic states were not, according to Islamic law, to be deprived of protection of life, property or freedom of religion. They *{ahl al-dhimma* or *dhimmis)* were, on the other hand, accorded membership in the Islamic state under a social contract. They were called *al-mu'ahadun*, which means contractees or holders of the covenant, because they were granted membership in the state through contracts concluded between them or their ancestors and the Islamic state (muslim majority)...In short, the non-Muslim minorities were allowed to continue those practices proper to their ethnicity or religion, and were not forced to assimilate into the dominant majority, ie. become Muslims. As *dhimma,* they entered into membership in the state on a contractual basis; their existence as a nation or ethny was legally recognized by the state. The state did not provide financial support for non-Muslim cultural traditions, but neither did it require taxes *(zakat)* from these communities although it was required from the Muslim majority. These communities were left to levy their own taxes for the benefit of their own community. In essence, minority communities continued to function as nations, conducting normal business with each other and with the

majority (except for the practice of usury. Also "foreign relations" insofar as it concerned politics and military protection remained the province of the Muslim majority.)" Y. N. Kly, The Anti-Social Contract, Clarity Press, Atlanta, 1985.

260 Both numbers and relative power are factors in determining whether a particular group should be considered a "minority". Deschênes, "Proposal concerning a definition of the term 'minority'", E/CN.4/Sub.2/1985/31.

261 Capotorti, Study on the Rights of Persons Belonging to Ethnic, Religious and Linguistic Minorities, pp. 1-2 (United Nations Publication Sales No. E.78.XIV.1).

262 De Azcarate, League of Nations and National Minorities, Carnegie, 1969.

263 Minority Schools in Albania, P.C.I.J. Ser. A/B, No. 64 (1935)

264 Millet in Ottoman law, which could apply to any autonomous religious or ethnic community.

265 The treaty with Italy refers to minorities in Trieste and the South Tyrol.

266 E/CN.4/367 and Add. 1 (1947).

267 Economic and Social Council resolutions (5(I) of 16 February 1946 and 9(II) of 26 June; (E/CN.4/Sub.2/8).

268 General Assembly resolution 217 D (III) of 10 December 1948.

269 Commission resolution 1 (A) (V) of 16 May 1949.

270 Sub-Commission resolution E(III), (E/CN.4/641).

271 Official Records of the General Assembly, Sixteenth Session (1961), A/5000 paras. 116-126. Article 27 has been paraphrased in the recently completed draft Convention on the Rights of the Child (E/CN.4/1989/29, Article 30), with the addition of the phrase, "or persons of indigenous origin."

272 Study of the Definition of Prevention of Discrimination and Protection of Minorities, E/CN.4/Sub.2/6; Definition and Classification of Minorities, U.N. Sales Publication No. 50 XIV.2; Provisions for Protection of Minorities, E/CN.4/Sub.2/L.43.

273 Sub-Commission resolution 9(XX), para. 198, E/CN.4/947.

274 Capotorti, op. cit.; Commission resolution 14 A (XXXIV) of 6 March 1978.

275 Report of the Working Group on the Rights of Persons Belonging to National, Ethnic, Religious and Linguistic Minorities, E/Cn.4/1989/36.

276 E/CN.4/Sub.2/31 and Corr. 1; Sub-Commission resolution 1985/6 of 28 August 1985.

277 E/CN.4/1986/43/para. 12.

278 E/CN.4/1986/43, Annex, p. 1.

279 Also the lack of such a program is emphasized by the lack of standard of well-defined definition of such key terms as discrimination, even in key civil rights acts. On page 22 of the Bakke Case syllabus, op. cit., Justices Brennan, White and Blackmun issued the following statement: "Indeed, there was a strong emphasis throughout Congress' consideration of Title VI on providing the Executive Branch with considerable flexibility in interpreting and applying the prohibition against racial discrimination. Attorney General Robert Kennedy testified that regulations had not been written into the legislation itself because the rules and regulations defining discrimination might differ from one program to another so that the term would assume different meanings in different contexts."

280 Milner S. Ball, "Judicial Protection of Powerless Minorities," Iowa Law Review, Vol. 59, No. 5, 1977, pp. 1059—95. Here, the author of the article discussed the ideas of James Madison, Alexander Hamilton and Thomas Jefferson on the constitutional and U.S. systemic approach to minority protection in light of current Supreme Court decisions and civil rights legislation dealing with national minorities and others.

281 See Introduction to this research. 1900-60 saw the periods in which the major European powers were, above all, involved in intra-continental warfare and consequently called to the U.S. for military and economic assistance and eventually political leadership. It was the period in which the U.S. rose to its zenith in relation to other powers and in so doing, practically controlled the direction of the international environment.

282 See Chapter 4. Also note that even anti-slavery sentiment was preceded by England's efforts to have the U.S. adopt the 1824 anti-slavery treaty.

283 In order for elements I-III to be operative, it is necessary for the majority ethny to maintain political and economic domination over the minority ethny.

284 In this concept majority interest and national interest are seen as identical.

285 This function is governed or made possible by the political and economic domination over time of the minority, and is an historically-observed consistent component of all relevant past events.

286 At numerous points in this research, we have called attention to assimilation as being the reported ideal goal of the post slavery and post apartheid USVCR. However, whatever the goal was said to be, the actual USVCR as defined above remained the same. We have assumed that the goal, as reported and interpreted is the goal of assimilation. Some authors mentioned felt that the goal is neo-colonialism, etc.. We accepted the official goal as voiced by the U.S. government in its report to the Sub-Commission.

287 At each historical occasion when minority rights became an issue, a solution was attempted by increasing the degree to which black Americans were legally given the same rights as Anglo-Americans, or by increasing their assimilation in the majority ethny.

288 It is the various secondary minority rights (see Part One, Chapter 5) made applicable by the general principle (ILVCR) that actually tend to define and fix the rights of minorities for the purpose of international protection.

289 This permanent recognition prevents minority rights from being rescinded by states upon any conflict of same with the interest of the majority, an occurrence which we observed in the preceding section, where rights were extended to or rescinded from the black minority in the U.S. according to fluctuations in the Anglo-American majority interest.

290 E/CN.4/Sub-2l384lAdd. 5, p. 10.

291 E/CN.4/Sub.2/384/Add. 5, p. 20.

292 Conférence sur la securité et la cooperation en Europe, Act final, loc. cit..

293 An example: While a number of colleges did institute black American Study Programs following the riots of 1963-68, these programs, having not been made permanent in law as special measures for the protection of the black minority culture in the U.S., now are in the process of being dismantled.

294 While we have suggested that in several state practices immigrant minorities are generally expected to assimilate, the ILVCR as represented in Article 27 of the Covenant on Civil and Political rights does not yet distinguish between national and immigrant minorities for the purpose of international protection.

295 E/CN.4/Sub.2/384/Add. 3, p. 31.

296 E/CN.4/Sub.2/384/Add. 1, p. 69.

297 E/CN.4/Sub.2/384/Add. 5, p. 9.

298 E/CN.4/Sub.2/384/Add. 5, p. 10.

299 E/CN.4/Sub.2/384/Add. 3, p. 31

300 Boutros-Ghali, Cultural Rights as Human Rights, (SCH. 68/XIX 3/a) UNESCO, Paris, 1970, p. 13. Also see E/CN.4/Sub.2/384/Add. 4, p. 11.

301 Recently, there are some very concrete as well as theoretical indications of this possibility. For concrete indications, see Congressional Record Proceedings and Debates of the 95th Congress Second Session, Vol. 124, No. 18, Washington, D.C., February 24, 1978, speech by the Honorable Walter E. Fauntroy of the Distnct of Columbia, House of Representatives.

302 Richard Falk, in The Rights of Indigenous Peoples in International Law, Ruth Thompson, ed., Unviersity of Saskatchewan Native Law Center, p. 60, 1987.

303 Jean-Jacques Rousseau, Du Contrat Social, edited by R.G. Schwartzenberg, Editions Seghers, Paris, 1971, p. 110.

304 U.N. Doc. E/CN.2/Sub.4/284, Add. 1977. A full reading of these documents shows that such minorities, while having been discussed, are not recognized as minorities requiring special protection under Article 27.

305 See Convention on the Political Rights of Women; Convention on Consent to Marriage, Minimum Age for Marriage and Registration of Marriages, etc.. A Compilation of International Instruments of the United Nations, U.N. Publication, New York, 1973.

306 E/CN.4/Sub.2/384/Add. 1. The section of this document listing the minorities found in various multi-national countries makes this statement regarding the U.S..

307 Boutros-Ghali, Cultural Rights as Human Rights, Paris UNESCO, 1970 (SHC68/ XIX.3/A), p. 100. In general, the author deals with the problem of culture in relation to assimilation, immigrant minorities and provision of protection for cultural preservation. U.N. document entitled "Definition of Minorities for Purposes of Protection" by the United Nations, recognizes that not all minority groups pose problems of protection when the group in question seeks complete identity with the rest of the population, etc..

308 Although France officially sees itself as a single ethny, it was suggested in the Sub-Commission Special Report on Minorities that in actuality France consists of certain national minorities, the most commonly known is the Breton minority. See E/CN.4/Sub.2/384/Add.

309 In the Algerian-French cease-fire agreement, Algerians of French civil status were guaranteed the right to preserve their own culture if they so desired. See Journal Officiel de la République Française, no 67, March 20, 1962.